A Tale of Two Trips

Travelling Around California
in a Motorhome

Chris Handy

Copyright © 2014 Chris Handy

All rights reserved, including the right to reproduce this book, or portions thereof in any form. No part of this text may be reproduced, transmitted, downloaded, decompiled, reverse engineered, or stored, in any form or introduced into any information storage and retrieval system, in any form or by any means, whether electronic or mechanical without the express written permission of the author.

ISBN: 978-1-291-71874-4

PublishNation. London

www.publishnation.co.uk

This book is dedicated to:

My late wife, for her understanding, support and love, and to my travelling companion who made both trips so enjoyable and rewarding.

Table of Contents

Chapter 1: Song to the Siren *(With Apologies to Robert Plant)* 1

Chapter 2: It Started with a Kiss (*With Apologies to Hot Chocolate*) 3

Chapter 3: Go, Go, Go! (*With Apologies to Murray Walker*)..11

    Map of Trip 1..11

Chapter 4: Are You Going to San Francisco? (*With Apologies to Scott McKenzie and the Mamas and Papas*).......................22

Chapter 5: (Almost) On the Road Again (*With apologies to Canned Heat*)..29

Chapter 6: The Long and Winding Road (*With Apologies to the Beatles*)..37

Chapter 7: Lazing on A Sunny Afternoon (*With Apologies to the Kinks*) 42

Chapter 8: Born to be Wild (*With Apologies to Steppenwolf*)..50

Chapter 9: Down in the Valley Below (*With Apologies to Led Zeppelin*) 56

Chapter 10: Slippin' And Slidin' (*With Apologies to Buddy Holly*)..62

Chapter 11: The Sky is Crying (*With apologies to Elmore James, Clarence Lewis, and Morris Levy*)..................69

Chapter 12: I'm Going Home (*With Apologies to Ten Years After*)..77

Chapter 13: Back Home Again (*With Apologies to John Denver*)..81

Chapter 14: San Franciscan Nights (*With Apologies to Eric Burdon and the Animals*) 87

Map of Trip 2..87

Chapter 15: Going Up The Country (*With Apologies to Canned Heat*) 99

Chapter 16: Yosemite Sam (*With Apologies to Mel Blanc*)..105

Chapter 17: Up Around the Bend (*With Apologies to Creedence Clearwater Revival*) 116

Chapter 18: Viva Las Vegas (*With Apologies to Elvis*)..127

Chapter 19: Pacific Coast Highway (*With Apologies to the Mamas and Papas*)..136

Chapter 20: Run For Home (*With apologies to Lindisfarne*)..141

Chapter 21: Reminiscing (*With Apologies to Buddy Holly*)..146

Appendix I – Selected Recipes from the Trip 150

Chapter 1: Song to the Siren
(With Apologies to Robert Plant)

I could hear the sound of the sirens. The sound was getting closer; now starting to come around the perimeter road. I went out to meet them. The ambulance screeched to a halt and the sirens went silent.

The driver got out and asked me, "Where's the patient?"

"That's me," I wheezed back.

Ten minutes before, I had visited the reception of the RV park (In the UK we would call an RV a motor-home and an RV park a campsite) to enquire how I might contact a local doctor, only to be told, "You've got a cell (mobile phone) haven't you? Call 911".

I explained that I just had a chest infection and needed to get some antibiotics from a doctor and didn't need an ambulance or trip to a hospital, just an appointment with a doctor - tomorrow would do! I was told, firmly, that in the US seeing a doctor was accomplished by dialling 911, so, disbelievingly, I did.

I asked for an ambulance and got put through to the Fire Department. I apologised for contacting the wrong emergency service and explained that I needed an ambulance. The operator told me that the Fire Department ran the ambulance service; what was the emergency? I explained about the chest infection, and that all I wanted was to see a doctor, and that it wasn't an emergency. I even told the operator that I thought it was odd that I had been advised to call 911 as it wasn't an emergency and the UK ambulance service would be mightily upset to come out for a simple chest infection!

"The ambulance will be with you shortly," was her reply.

I guess that in America they have to despatch an ambulance once you have called. True to her words, the ambulance was there in less than ten minutes, closely followed by a fire engine! As I would have expected their British counterparts to be, they were not amused to be called out for a chest infection. I explained that it wasn't my idea, and that reception had advised calling 911 despite my protests. The paramedics were extremely sympathetic in the circumstances and gave me a map to the nearest emergency doctor and promised to have a 'word' with reception on their way out.

It had all started two years earlier in a small town in Southern England...

Chapter 2: It Started with a Kiss
(With Apologies to Hot Chocolate)

In 2004 we were invited to a meeting at my son's school where we were given a presentation about a proposed school trip touring America. It was to be sixteen days long and covered a large portion of the US. We were shown pictures of previous trips to the US by the school and it looked to be the trip of a lifetime for a teenager. Sixteen days with your schoolmates; sixteen days in a foreign country; sixteen days in the country seen only in films so far; sixteen days away from Mum and Dad!

It was explained to us that, as it was an expensive trip, we were being told about it two years in advance so that we could participate in the school trip 'savings scheme', where we paid in an amount each month and, when the trip happened a couple of years in the future, we would have already paid for it.

Several years before (when my son, Adam, was three), we lost our dog and had decided not to take on the responsibility of another dog. We no longer had anyone to look after a dog if we wanted to go abroad since our respective parents had gotten older and we were still feeling the pain from the loss of our old companion.

However, it soon became plain that Adam was missing his old pal, and one day my wife, Simone, saw a litter of dogs and fell in love with one of them. She came home to discuss with us the possibility of taking on her new found love.

Adam was keen to have another dog and so Simone and I decided that if we were going to do so, we would spend the money that we would have spent on foreign holidays and buy a caravan and then use it not only for our annual holidays, but for any weekends that we could get away and we could take the dog with us.

As a result of this decision, we had many superb holidays and weekends away. We saw wonderful countryside, and met friendly people in Cornwall, Wales, Norfolk and South East England. However Adam was not exposed to foreign travel like his peers and so missed out on exposure to other cultures, climates, food and scenery.

It was a lot of money, but the trip looked exciting and educational, and Adam was keen to go. We felt that it would be a good opportunity for Adam to experience more of the world and we paid our deposit. Shortly afterwards, we received a letter to say that interest was not as great as had been hoped, and that it may cost a little more as there were fewer students going; did we still want to participate? As Adam was so keen and we thought that it would be good for his education, we agreed. We were sent a savings card and started shelling out each month.

Fifteen months later we received another letter to tell us that several students had dropped out and that the trip was no longer financially viable. Who did we want the refund cheque made payable to? That was simple - me!

What was not so easy to deal with was Adam's and our disappointment. He'd been looking forward to seeing something of the world, and visiting America. For a fifteen year old boy, Adam had (and still has) a highly developed political and social conscience and was well aware of the effects of American foreign policy, especially in relation to the 'War on Terrorism' and, more specifically, the invasion of Iraq. He didn't like what the US had done and vehemently disagreed with George Bush Junior's policies. This had translated into a distrust of all Americans, and I was hoping that a visit to the US would show him that a country's political leader's views did not necessarily coincide with the views of the general population. I think that Adam was looking forward to telling any American citizen that he met what he thought of their leader, their country, their society and, especially their foreign policy!

The next question was, "What we were going to do with the refund money?' Should we spend it on a new car, new furniture, a new carpet or just put it in a savings account for a 'rainy day'? The answer was obvious, really. The money had been 'saved' for Adam to have an educational trip, so that's what it would be used for!

The next question was - Where to?' The original trip had been grand in scope but the money was only to finance one person's travel. Depending on the trip chosen, it would now have to finance at least two people's travel (Adam being too young to travel abroad on his own). Adam was consulted.

His first plan was to undertake a survival course with British bush-craft and survival expert Ray Mears. This would have involved him in learning 'bush-craft' skills and camping rough for a week. Adam had long had an interest in the outdoors, wildlife, and generally-forgotten backwoods skills and was very comfortable in an outdoors environment. A survival course would have been an ideal way to spend the money...except that it would only spend some of the money, and would be located in the UK.

Part of the criteria that Simone and I had for the disposition of the money was that any trip had to have an educational component, and be in another country so that Adam could experience a different culture. We thought that the survival course would qualify on the educational front, but not on the 'other cultures' front, so further ideas were sought. Adam was keen to do a safari in Africa and I would have been happy to go to the Far East.

By now we had more or less decided that it would be just Adam and I that went on the trip to make the budget spread further and Simone would be able look after the dog whilst we were away. We looked at prices for Africa and the Far East but they were way over our budget!

I have never taken a package holiday as I don't like the idea of being herded around and having my itinerary decided for me. I like to decide where I go, when I go there and reserve the right to change my mind according to what I discover whilst travelling. This summer we went to the Lake District (where Adam, at last, undertook his hoped-for five day survival course) and whilst he was 'surviving', Simone and I took a cruise on Lake Windermere.

On the cruise we met a party of Australians who were on a coach tour of the UK. Their comments showed what I think are the worst of packaged holidays: "After the cruise we are going to go to a gift shop, and then, this afternoon, we're off to Gretna Green." I don't want to be shepherded to a 'gift shop' that is most likely to be paying a 'commission' to the tour company, and I would like to have the flexibility to spend more time in an area I find I like (such as, perhaps, the Lake District?). The trips to Africa and the Far East were also package tours, and therefore not very desirable to me. When I researched going independently, it looked to be just as expensive, if not more so, and required horrendously complicated travel arrangements and visas.

So it was back to the idea of visiting America. In terms of pounds per mile, America is a comparatively cheap country to travel to and there are few paperwork problems, especially since I had an indefinite multiple entry visa. Despite the old adage that "America and the UK are two countries separated by a common language", there are few language problems and arranging accommodation is easy and cheap. Couple that with a good exchange rate and a lower cost of living compared to the UK and our 'one into two' budget could be made to stretch a little further.

Additionally, the US was Adam's original destination, so it ticked all the educational and cultural boxes – but where in America? The US is a large country and our budget would not extend to the grand tour, covering several states, that his school had originally intended?

I had a work colleague that had taken a sabbatical year to tour the world and I asked for his opinion. After several discussions he recommended a visit to Yosemite National Park in California. This seemed an ideal place for us to visit. It fitted well with our collective interest in the outdoors, has a good climate and the locals have a great attitude. Web research showed that the best airport for Yosemite, when flying from the UK, was San Francisco International.

Before Adam was born, I had visited California on business. My colleagues and I had spent a long weekend in San Francisco, being shown the sights by the MD of our sister company over there, and I had liked what I had seen. Trips to other companies across California furthered my interest. The variety of landscapes and the friendly people fascinated me. Adam was intrigued by the stories of my visit and so it was decided: California it would be!

With the decision made, I started to look for flights, and almost as soon as I did, British Airways announced a sale, which seemed like a good omen. I found a great rate for San Francisco, providing that we departed on the last day of Adam's school term. Going the next day would have added an extra £130 per person to the airfare. This was a big decision for us. Simone and I had only ever taken Adam out of school for one day before, the day of my graduation. I'd completed a degree as a mature student when Adam was twelve and we felt that going to see his Dad's graduation would encourage him at school, so felt that was justified. We agonised over this proposed school absence for a while before reasoning that the trip was educational, and that not much was learned on the last day of school term. Also, £260 was a significant chunk of money from our budget, so we would go for it! I booked the flights without delay before BA could change their minds!

Next we had to work out where we were going to stay. As we wanted to tour around California, we decided to see if we could rent a motor-home. We were accustomed to touring with a caravan, but they are few and far between in the US where motor-homes are more prevalent, so a motor-home it would be.

It took many hours on the web to find a suitable rental near to San Francisco, but eventually I did. Plans at this time were still 'flexible' so I requested quotes for several options in terms of time, mileage and degree of comfort. The degree of comfort encompassed both type and length of motor-home and additional options such as bedding and cooking utensils. As we were planning to go wild camping in Yosemite, we would be taking basic camp cooking utensils and bedding, so we could potentially have used these in the motor-home.

When the quotes came back, they were from the rental company's UK office, which was less than a mile for my workplace! To save time, I visited during my lunch break and booked the motor-home there and then, taking the basic package with no optional extras. The rental company offered a free shuttle service from selected San Francisco hotels to the motor-home pick-up, which was a big plus point in their favour as far as we were concerned; however, it did mean that we would have to spend a night in a San Francisco hotel before collecting the motor-home. We picked what looked to be an interesting hotel from their list, which had a 'films set in San Francisco' theme and booked that for our first night in California. By mid December 2005 we had our flights, accommodation and travel insurance booked (more of the travel insurance later!).

As you will find, if you decide to keep on reading, Adam and I were subjected to several events that we hadn't planned for, most notably my health and problems with the rented motor-homes: Yes motor-homes – plural! These events changed the course and nature of our trip, but also, in some way, made the trip. It has been said that it is the journey and not the destination that is enjoyable, and so it was for us.

The enforced changes in our itinerary meant that we saw things we would otherwise have missed, and having seen them, I'm glad that we did. We met an amazing variety of friendly, caring and helpful people whom we would not have met if we had a problem-free trip. Finally, we got a discount off the motor-home rental because of the problems we experienced, and because my health prevented us from achieving the primary aim on this trip, we later decided to come back again the following year.

Had we have been on a package tour, things would not have worked out so well. I doubt that being on a package trip would have made any difference to the motor-home problems, or their resolution, but my health would have probably curtailed the trip entirely. Take heed, don't be afraid to 'go it alone', there is more to be gained than lost, and finding and booking transport and accommodation is easier than ever with the internet!

However that was all in the future. We were still planning on camping in Yosemite, so I scoured the January sales for the equipment that we would need. We had been wild camping before, so were reasonably sufficient in equipment, but the preceding flight and different conditions in California, meant that we needed to add to our existing inventory.

One thing that we would need to buy over there was a stove as the airlines prohibit the transportation of fuel and we were not certain that we would be able to get the correct gas cylinders for our UK stoves in the US. I ended up buying a new rucksack for myself (the old one was uncomfortable), a few odds and ends and some iodine-based water purifying tablets that were safe for use in areas with giardia, a parasite of the small intestine, not found in the UK but prevalent in Yosemite. Our existing chlorine-based water purification tablets, whilst fine for the UK, did not kill the giardia parasite, so iodine it had to be. I also bought several travel books relating to Yosemite, California, San Francisco and Los Angeles.

One thing that concerned me about wild camping in Yosemite was the possibility of meeting a wild black bear. Black bears in Yosemite have learned that where there are humans there is food: in trash cans; in coolers; in cars and so on. The bears, being rather large and powerful, are able to inflict serious, and often fatal, damage to humans. They can rip open the metal skin of a car with their claws to get at any food inside and are also attracted to anything perfumed, such as soap or toothpaste.

A bear features on the California State Flag with good reason! The books and the websites advised that we should rent a bear canister from Yosemite Village to keep food and perfumed stuff in; in fact it's a legal requirement to use a bear canister when backpacking in Yosemite. These canisters are sometimes called 'bear footballs' due to their shape (similar to an American football) and the bear's habit of kicking them around in an effort to get at the contents. It would also be necessary to put all food and perfumed items from the motor-home in a free of charge bear locker. These are available at most trail heads to stop the bears 'breaking into' motor-homes. Knowing how to prevent bears targeting us, and having discovered the fact that most bear attacks were in car parks, made me feel more comfortable!

Research continued throughout February and March for our end of March departure and we formulated a rough plan for our two weeks over Easter in California. After our first night in a hotel in San Francisco, we would collect the motor-home and then return to an RV park in San Francisco to spend a day and a couple of nights there. From San Francisco, we would go to Yosemite and spend four days there (three wild camping) and then tour down to Los Angeles, where we would spend a few days before heading back up the coast to San Francisco to return the motor-home, which would mean a journey of almost 1000 miles. This was not what would happen . . .

About ten days before departure, two things happened. Firstly I got a cold, and secondly we were watching TV when a travel program came on featuring Charley Boorman of 'Excalibur', 'The Emerald Forest', 'Long Way Round', and 'Long Way Down' fame, showcasing a holiday touring California on a motorcycle. Prior to Adam being born, I had been a keen, nay avid motorcyclist, but the arrival of a young son meant that I had to be more of a family man and the motorcycle(s) went. The urge and passion to ride one didn't, however!

Charley Boorman gave me an idea . . . we could hire a bike for a day or so whilst we were in California! Adam was old enough to be on the back of a bike and what could be more natural than riding an 'iron horse' in the US of A? More web research followed and I identified a few motorcycle rental places. I was reluctant to make a firm booking as I wanted to leave our schedule open; however, I printed the details to take with me.

The packing list had long since been drawn up and we were ready to start the process. It was like packing for two trips; one a camping trip, and another a normal holiday. We were ready to start the actual packing when my cold got worse and I had to take some time off work. I started to wonder if I would be fit enough for the trip. I had travel insurance, so with a Doctor's note I would be able to claim most of the money back, but the flights had been booked in a sale, and getting other flights at the same price would be difficult.

As the departure date grew nearer, I was slowly starting to get better, and I decided to bite the bullet and go. Even though I wasn't one hundred percent fit, I was on the mend and hoped that I would continue to feel progressively better when we got to America. I went back to work for the last day before departure as it doesn't look good to be off sick the day before going on holiday! We were ready for the off, but what would lie in store for us in California?

Chapter 3: Go, Go, Go!

(With Apologies to Murray Walker)

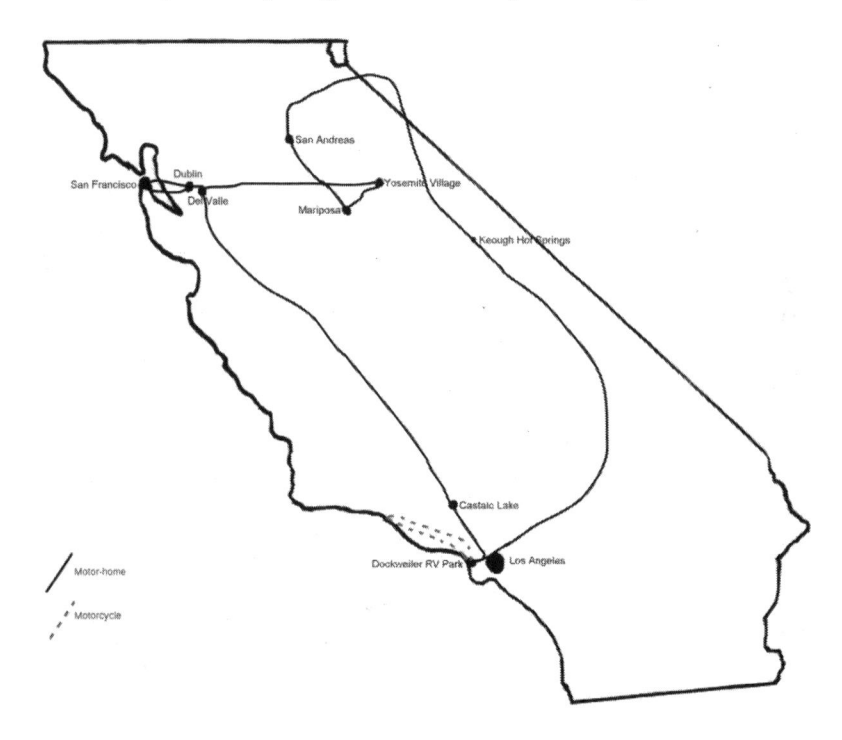

Map of Trip 1

Thursday 30th March dawned clear and we were excitedly ready for the off. I was feeling better than I had for about two weeks and we were ready for anything (or so we thought!). We were booked on the 13:50 flight and Simone dropped us off at Heathrow in good time. We each had a brand new wheeled suitcase and a large rucksack. I'd taken advantage of the on-line check in the night before and reserved our seats. However, when we arrived, we discovered that I'd requested seats in different rows, one behind the other (I got confused with the seat numbering system!). That was soon remedied by the helpful lady from British Airways and Adam and I were able to get seats adjacent to each other.

Adam had only flown on an airliner once before, when he was three, so was quite excited to be flying all the way to California. However, the boredom of international, long distance air travel soon set in.

Being six feet two inches tall, and generally a 'big bloke', I'm not a great fan of long distance flights either. I spend the whole time with my knees wedged into the back of the seat in front and it can be somewhat painful if the person in front decides to recline their seat!

Ideally I'd like to be able to sleep, as this would relieve the boredom and go some way to combating jet lag; however, the uncomfortable seating position, coupled with the usual screaming kids, means that I never seem to be able to properly drop off and so arrive stiff and tired. I generally try to get an aisle seat so that I can stretch my legs in the aisle when the flight attendants are not serving food or drinks and it's also easier to get up and have a wander around.

However, Adam, new to air travel, wanted a window seat, and so I ended up in the middle seat. He soon found out that there's not a lot to see once you reach cruising altitude and succumbed to boredom and began surfing the in-flight entertainment.

Several years later (or so it seemed), the flight landed and we had to undergo the usual immigration checks. Adam had completed his visitor's visa form on the plane and I had my indefinite, multiple entry visa in my old passport. We finally made it to the front of the queue and presented our documents. "What's this?" the immigration official asked pointing to my visa. "My visa" I replied. "Why have you got a multiple entry indefinite visa?" he asked. "Because when I came over to the US on business in 1986 I needed a visa and this is the one that they gave me". Bang, Bang, Bang went the stamp on my passport, "I'm revoking it" said the official, you'll need to complete a visitor's visa form next time. I looked at my passport and it had the word 'CANCELLED' in big red letters all over the visa stamps. Underneath it had a smaller stamp "Revoked under section 221(i) cancelled without prejudice". Checking on the web after my return, I found that Section 221(i) refers to potential terrorists and allows the authorities to deport you at any time!

We'd booked shuttle transport to the hotel and as I was loading my new suitcase into the bus, the handle snapped. Fortunately, it was one of those suitcases that have a handle on the side and the top, so there was still something to grab on to. It was just an inconvenience really and I got a full refund after we returned to the UK.

The hotel was situated in an area of San Francisco called the Tenderloin. I'd booked before doing too much research on San Francisco, mainly basing my hotel choice on the list provided by the RV rental company.

When I did do the research, it showed that the Tenderloin is part of one of the rougher areas of San Francisco: *"... the Tenderloin is a down town bruise that never seems to heal. It's an entire neighbourhood of skid rows, each lined with near identical apartments inhabited by the downtrodden and nearly homeless. Prostitutes and drug dealers walk some of the streets. Deranged souls wander into the oncoming traffic."*[1]

After reading the guide books and talking to the shuttle driver, I was starting to feel a little apprehensive about the district that we were to stay in, but we found the locals to be friendly. Sure, there were a lot of homeless people begging on the street, but all were well mannered and accepted a polite refusal with good grace. We never felt threatened. I truly felt sorry for some of these people, but there were simply too many to give something to each of them, and I therefore felt it was fairer to give to none. I'm sure that if I had given to one, we would have been accosted by every other beggar in sight and I couldn't face having to refuse them.

San Francisco has a large homeless population, due to the historical political practice of distributing money to the homeless of San Francisco. Attitudes have now changed and a new program 'Care not Cash' has been instituted where less cash is distributed to the homeless and the cash saved is invested in shelters. A year after its introduction, there were 800 people in the shelters, but this is a drop in the ocean compared with the estimated 12,000 living rough on the streets.

The hotel we had booked, The Bijou, is a 'boutique hotel' being themed on films shot in or around San Francisco and incorporating a

---

1 Tom Downs, San Francisco City Guide, Lonely Planet 2006, p71

small cinema where they showed a selection of these films. The staff were friendly and helpful and soon had us settled in room 307, which was themed on the film *"When a Man Loves a Woman"* starring Meg Ryan and Andy Garcia (not that I've ever seen it!). The room was clean and well equipped, if not overly large.

After a quick shower and change, we headed out to find some dinner as it was now early evening. Our plan was to have a wander around and find a restaurant that appealed. After a short walk and looking at half a dozen menus we settled on 'John's Grill'. This is the restaurant made famous by the author Dashiell Hammett in his book 'The Maltese Falcon'. In the book the hero, Sam Spade, orders "chops, baked potato and sliced tomato" in John's Grill. The restaurant has been open since 1908 and the walls, which are clad in dark oak panelling, reflect this long history. They are covered in pictures of the great and the good who have eaten there. As would be expected many are film stars but there are also presidents and sports stars up there on the walls too.

Whilst we were dining, a guy set up a stool and amp and started to play jazz guitar. His wonderful laid back guitar licks set the perfect mood for the meal and the forthcoming trip. Adam and I were entranced and had a coffee after the meal just so that we could listen for a little longer. However before long jet lag got the better of us, well of me anyway, and we set off back to the hotel.

We'd been up for about twenty two hours by this time so I had no difficulty getting to sleep, However, as is often the case with jet lag, Adam and I awoke early, at about three in the morning, as our body clocks hadn't yet adjusted to local time!

We lay awake intermittently talking about yesterday's events and our forthcoming plans and trying to get back to sleep. By four thirty we'd had enough and got up to go for a walk and search for some breakfast. We walked around Union Square and then found an all night café just a hundred or so yards from the Hotel. Since Supertramp sang so eloquently about "Breakfast in America", we decided to go for the full American breakfast. Adam particularly enjoyed the pancakes in syrup which were a first for him.

Adam recalls his time in San Francisco thus:

"My first night spent in America tasted good. We arrived in San Francisco after my first memorable plane flight, (I had flown to

France once, but I was only a baby and I slept through most of it anyway), and after settling at our Hotel we went to a steakhouse. Now, in Britain, a steakhouse is basically a pub that serves a lot of tough, lukewarm steak with onion rings and chips, as I'm sure you're familiar with. This particular one was an American steakhouse, and an upmarket, famous one, apparently. We hadn't realised it until we walked in. The only hint until we entered was the prices on the menu, but luckily Dad was up for eating there too, so we did. It turned out that many famous faces had eaten there. I can't remember any of them at all, and they weren't "Celebrities" as we know them today, (egotistical young people who get paid a lot of money for not a lot, while cameramen and journalists set up camp on their doorstep), but people who made good music or did something important, or were particularly successful, etc. The steak was magical, thick and tender with sour cream and a baked potato. Now I have always found baked potato bland and unappealing but with sour cream it was good, and it goes with steak well. Americans have strange food ideas but many of them are good, or at least worth the novelty of trying it out. (For instance, they have this stuff known as Steak Sauce, which is basically Brown sauce mixed with Worcester sauce. It tastes good on steak too.) Due to Jet-lag we didn't sleep that night and so at roughly 4:00 AM local time we found ourselves in an all night café eating Mexican food, which was also good, but no cigar compared with the steak. I overdid it on the Tabasco, which is found in higher strengths and in more eateries in America than here. Therefore I had to face the arch nemesis of my teeth to try and cool my tongue down – over iced soft drinks. Over here, we call it an iced drink if it has say, 3 or 4 cubes of frozen H²0. In America, the phrase "With no ice" holds about as much weight as Kate Moss' shoes. They aren't satisfied until only about a third of what's in the glass is what you paid for, by the glass. Effectively this means soft drinks are roughly 3 times too expensive, and toothpaste brands in America offering "sensitive teeth" treatment must be very happy. For the record, the steakhouse had an amazing jazz guitarist playing in the upstairs room (where we were), and the café was on O' Farrell Street, San Francisco."

I rang El Monte RV (the people who we were renting the motorhome from) to arrange for the transfer to their premises in Dublin (about 35 miles East of San Francisco). We were told that the shuttle bus would be with us between 11:30 and 12:30. The hotel staff were confident in their prediction that the bus would be late, but at 11:40 the shuttle bus showed up and an affable Bulgarian loaded our luggage and we set off towards Dublin. The Bulgarian driver was friendly and chatty and the trip passed quickly.

To get out of San Francisco we went over Bay Bridge, which links San Francisco with Oakland on the other side of the bay and is the longest steel bridge in the world. It's in two sections divided by Yerba Buena Island and, in total, is nearly 8.5 miles long! The views over the bay were superb and we were able to see Alcatraz in the distance as we travelled across the bridge. The day was sunny and we enjoyed our first views of rural California. We soon discovered that, despite being a state in the prosperous United States of America, the Californian roads are poorly maintained. The bus rattled and shook as it hit pot holes, ridges and bumps in the road, at times the rattles drowned out the music on the stereo and made conversation difficult. Welcome to America!

As we pulled off the Interstate into Dublin our Bulgarian friend was pointing out the cheapest gas (petrol) stations and the best supermarkets for stocking up on necessary provisions. The check-in was slick in the way that American organisation is. We started with a short video, showing us how to use the many facilities and features of the motor-home, then we signed the paperwork, checked over the vehicle and were shown how to operate the various appliances in person.

When I booked I'd declined the additional extra packs such as bedding and cooking utensils as we were taking sleeping bags and cooking kit for our camping trip, but seeing the packs laid out in the showroom I decided that we might as well live in comfort and added these to our bill (it's only money after all!). The whole process took about one and a half hours and then we were on our way to the supermarket to stock up on provisions.

Perhaps now would be a good time to say a few words about the motor-home we had hired, which I think I'll call an RV from now on, as it's the American term and fits with the spirit of the trip. In the UK a trailer caravan is by far the most common form of rigid camping accommodation, with RVs a distant second (take a look on any UK camp-site!). In America the reverse is true. There are far more RVs than trailer caravans. In addition there are '5th wheel' RVs which are similar to what in the UK we would call an articulated lorry. The motive power is provided by a pick-up truck with a large hitch mounted in the bed of the truck and the accommodation in a trailer behind. We had hired a twenty five foot RV, which in the UK would be considered medium to large, but in the US is definitely considered small. In fact the smallest!

In the UK, pitches with an electrical hook up are called 'premium pitches'. Water is carried to the caravan in a container, the most favoured being barrel-shaped so that they can be rolled along the ground with a handle to save lifting heavy water.

Waste water is similarly captured in another container and rolled to the nearest disposal point when full. The same is true of sewage, where the waste is collected in a container that forms part of the loo and can be sealed before being removed and carried to the emptying point (emptying the loo is the least popular job on a UK camp-site!).

In the US, it is most unusual to have a pitch that doesn't have electricity, mains water, a TV hook-up and a sewage outlet. For the few pitches that don't have hook-ups, RVs have fresh, grey (washing up and shower) and black (sewage) water tanks. You stop, connect all the services and have all the facilities of home. In fact since returning from the US, Adam has decided that he doesn't like UK caravanning any longer, describing it as "the hell of carting shit across a field".

I guess it's true to say that the only modern appliances missing from our RV were a dishwasher and a TV, and we could have had a TV if we'd paid a little extra as the RV already had a built in aerial (we decided against the TV; have you ever seen American TV?). There was air-conditioning, a heater, hot water, an oven, a hob, a microwave, a shower, a toilet, a fridge, a freezer, a radio, a CD player and even a generator for pitches without mains electric hook-up. You get the idea?

A typical UK RV is based on a commercial van of some kind, usually with a 2 or 2.5 litre engine and a manual gearbox. Our rental RV was based on a Chevy pick-up truck and had a 7.4 litre engine with an automatic gearbox, and was of course left hand drive. At twenty five feet long and eight feet wide it was a fair sized vehicle to park and to drive around on the wrong side of the road! Luckily

America is a country designed for cars, unlike the UK which is designed for horses and carriages!

There is also adequate parking with large bays at all shopping malls. Even so the RV usually took up two bays when we parked. Unlike UK RVs which have coil springs, the Dodge had leaf springs on the rear which meant that, coupled with the weight of the coachwork and domestic appliances, the handling was a lot less than perfect when going around bends. Fortunately Californian roads are mostly straight; unfortunately those that are not are up in the mountains, where missing a bend would probably resort in a rapid, off-road, uncontrolled descent!

It had one other frightening feature in that when gently applying the brakes on a downhill grade, the steering began to shake - violently. It never got to the uncontrollable point, and changing tyre pressures didn't seem to help, I just learned to live with it. Despite its shortcomings I became quite fond of the RV and found it a most luxurious way of camping in the wilds. The one thing that I didn't like was its fuel consumption. A 7.4 litre engine meant that the performance from such a large vehicle was, whilst not quick, at least adequate. However it did mean frequent stops at gas stations. Whilst gas was a fraction of the cost that it was in the UK, we did go through an enormous amount of it which simultaneously depleted both my wallet and the ozone layer.

How easy was it to drive? I found it surprisingly easy. It has power steering and an automatic gearbox. So two pedals, one to go and one to stop (don't be tempted to use one foot for each - use your right foot for both), and a steering wheel that is easy to turn. That's the good bit. I've driven a fair few vans, lorries and minibuses in my time and regularly tow a caravan, I'm used to driving large vehicles. If you're not, you have to bear in mind four things: -

1. ***The stopping distance.*** Although you don't tend to travel quickly in an RV, the weight of the vehicle makes stopping distances increase. Always look well ahead and anticipate when you may have to stop so that you can start slowing early. This also has the added advantage that a gentle controlled slowing down doesn't throw the contents of your motor-home against your head and empty cupboards in the same way that an emergency stop does!

2.   *Acceleration (or more precisely, the lack of it).* These things just don't accelerate. Think about this when you're waiting at a junction and the traffic seems endless. 'Nipping' out into a small gap isn't an option when you're driving a 25 foot (or longer) RV! Allow plenty of space when you pull out.

3.   *The size of the vehicle.* You need to be aware of the width. As the body is wider than the bonnet there's no guarantee that all of it will go through a tight gap just because the bonnet does! Also the length means that you need a wide turning circle to prevent the sides scraping on obstacles like trees and fence posts. You also need to remember the length when reversing and it's advisable to get someone to guide you back wherever possible. One thing that most people forget is that, with such a large length of vehicle hanging out behind the rear wheels, the rear of the RV can move slightly in the opposite direction to which you are turning. Expensive if you're close to something solid when you do it! As RVs are higher than most vehicles on the road, do memorise the height of yours (rental companies usually put a notice on the dashboard to remind you) and look out for height signs on low structures that you will be driving under, such as canopies on gas station forecourts and bridges.

4.   *Cornering.* It is the weight of the vehicle that extends braking distances and limits acceleration. This weight also reduces the cornering abilities of an RV. The fact that an RV carries its weight comparatively high (as a result of all the wonderful modern appliances and gadgets that they put in them) exacerbates the problem, causing the body of the RV to 'roll' excessively when cornering. This is true of all RVs and large vehicles, but especially American RVs which have leaf spring suspension. You will therefore need to brake earlier for bends and corner more slowly and carefully. As with braking, this has the added bonus of not throwing your belongings around the inside of the RV!

If you bear the above points in mind you should not have any trouble driving a reasonably sized RV in the US. Within a day or so you should have got the feel for it and it will come quite naturally to you in much the same way as it takes an hour or two to get used to a different car.

Having said a few words about the RV, I guess I should also say a few about Adam and myself. Adam was fourteen at the time we first went to California and was a thoughtful boy with a strong ethical and social conscience. As he grew, Adam had developed a love of wildlife and the countryside. He has always liked animals and, as we live on the edge of a small town in the Hampshire countryside, his playground was the local woods and on the large expanses of ground that the army used for training. As I share his enjoyment of the outdoors, we had many holidays in the wilder parts of the UK, and had undertaken a couple of wild camping expeditions on Dartmoor and the Brecon Beacons. It was our mutual love of the outdoors that drew us to Yosemite and California.

At fourteen Adam took after me in height, being tall for his age. Fortunately for him he didn't take after me in girth and was (and still is) quite slim. He had just started to grow his hair long, causing one of our friends to remark that "despite getting taller, the ends of his hair never get any further from the floor!" Again this is the antithesis of me, as I lost all of my hair with alopecia twenty years ago, and it never grew back.

At this time new interests were coming to the fore, principally music, and Adam had started to learn to play the bass guitar. Whilst we were away Adam said that his bass guitar was the thing he missed most about home! Another burgeoning interest was what I will call philosophy, for want of a better descriptive word. Adam had always had an interest in the people of this world, why they did the things that they did, how different cultures had different beliefs and so on. He had firm convictions on the rights and wrongs of things that he either read about or saw on the news. He abhorred racism and war and was particularly incensed about the west's invasion of Iraq, considering it wholly wrong, and totally blaming George Bush Junior. With these beliefs I thought that we were in for an interesting time in the USA.

What can I say about myself? I've just shown Adam the paragraphs I wrote about him and incorporated his suggested changes. He commented that it would be difficult to write about yourself, as you will always see yourself from a different perspective from the rest of the world. He's right of course but I'll give it a go!

Father and son in Los Angeles with our rented Harley Davidson

I've always liked the outdoors and until I was about 32 always rode a motorcycle despite having a car licence. Finances dictated the use of a car as you need a car with a baby and I couldn't afford a car and a motorcycle, but I missed riding! As mentioned earlier, I lost my hair in 1986 which was quite a shock as I'd always had long hair and a beard. However I got used to it and find that now the only hair I miss is my eyelashes and eyebrows as I'm prone to getting dust and sweat in my eyes - other than that I don't care that I'm bald. Physically I'm six foot two with eyes of blue and slightly overweight due to my love of food and cooking (never trust a thin chef!).

Shortly after we'd collected the RV I was reminded of Bob Dylan's words: 'A Hard Rain's Gonna Fall', however in our case it was to be more like 'A *Cold* Rain's Gonna Fall!'

Chapter 4: Are You Going to San Francisco?
(With Apologies to Scott McKenzie and the Mamas and Papas)

After collecting the RV we headed straight for the supermarket for provisions. I hadn't given it too much thought beforehand, and didn't have a shopping list, only the idea to 'stock up on stuff we like'. As we went around the supermarket, it dawned on me that we not only needed food, but also needed cleaning materials, loo roll, and all of the stuff that I take for granted in a well stocked kitchen such as garlic, herbs, salt, pepper and so forth.

We were starting with a blank canvas and I needed to fill it! The bill was over 300 dollars! On the advice of the checkout operator I signed up for a loyalty card as this gave me 10% off but even with the discount card, it was still only just under 300 dollars. It did however include beer from the Sierra Nevada brewery and wine from the San Fernando valley!

As we headed back towards San Francisco, I felt water dripping down my neck as we rounded a bend. It appeared that there was a leak somewhere. As it was getting late, I decided to carry on to San Francisco and return the RV later if the problem persisted. We got lost trying to find our selected RV park and spent some time driving around the suburbs, but we eventually found it and checked in.

The receptionist had his arm in a sling and I wondered if he'd been attacked by a customer when he told me how much my stay was going to cost - $110 for 2 nights - that's $55 per night which equalled approximately £35 at that time!

The RV park was all asphalt with marked bays and we were allocated a space (in most UK camp-sites you can select any empty pitch that takes your fancy). The park was located opposite Candlestick Park, the home of the San Francisco 49'ers football team, and close to the bay shore.

We spent some time levelling up the RV and connecting the services as they were all strange to us and then headed for the park shop to stock up on the things that I hadn't got at the supermarket (there's always something you forget isn't there?). We ate in the RV for the first night and I cooked chicken in a white wine and tarragon sauce.

I was glad to have full sized pans and a basic set of utensils instead of the small camping pans that we had brought with us. They weren't the same quality as our pans at home, so I found them quite difficult to use as they were quite thin metal and prone to 'hot spots'. The main bugbear for me was the cook's knife -, I've got sharper butter knives! I bought a decent one on the next day and took it home with me when we left!

The RV park had a shuttle bus to take us and other happy campers into the heart of San Francisco and we caught the 10.30 bus to the financial district. I'm not some deranged banker or accountant and normally I wouldn't bother to visit the financial district of a foreign city, and now I can't even remember why we got off there. Maybe it was the only place the shuttle stopped, or maybe it was because it's central, or maybe it's the only place the shuttle stops because it's central. Whatever the reason, that's where we ended up!

Not knowing whether the radio in the RV would have a CD player or a cassette, I had decided not to bring any recorded music and to buy something suitable in San Francisco. We'd also decided to get some clothes and trainers for Adam as they're generally cheaper in the US. I find that the general rule is that the cost of clothes in the US is approximately the same in dollars as it is in pounds, and (if I remember correctly) the exchange rate at the time was around 1.6 - 1.7 dollars to the pound. This equates to clothes costing a little less than two thirds of the equivalent in the UK.

Several pairs of jeans and a pair of trainers later, we headed for the Virgin Megastore to get some sounds. We bought eight or nine CDs to keep us going. Fortunately Adam and I share similar musical tastes and it wasn't too difficult to find music that we both liked. Adam was very keen to get a Nirvana CD, a band that I hadn't, until this trip, listened to at all. By the end of the trip I was quite a fan and, in my mind, Nirvana's music will always remind me of the trip.

Adam also bought some T-Shirts (including a Nirvana T-Shirt). The lady who served us was quite friendly and we got to chatting about where we came from and what our plans were in California. She thought that it sounded great, and admitted that she had never been out of the US. It seems amazing to us in Europe that only a small percentage of American citizens travel outside of continental USA. Estimates as to what percentage of US citizens hold a passport vary but the consensus seems to be around 20% - 22%. I'm sure that there are many reasons for this, but I think the two main reasons are that America is so large just about any kind of countryside, scenery or weather can be found without going outside of its borders at any time of the year, and that, because of its geographical location and size, any trip to another country is more of an undertaking for an American. In Europe it's easy and cheap to travel to countries that are comparatively close.

After our bout of shopping we became typical tourists in San Francisco and headed for the cable cars, intending to take a trip to Fisherman's Wharf. The weather was glorious as we headed for the Powell Street turnaround. When we arrived, there was a very long queue and no cable cars in sight. After waiting for five minutes or so at the end of the queue with no cable cars appearing, we headed for Powell Street Muni Metro and BART station hoping to find an alternate method of getting to Fisherman's Wharf.

Muni Metro is a light rail transport system with parts of the network below ground, parts above ground in street cars and also an above ground light railway (Muni are also responsible for running the cable cars in San Francisco.) It is run by the San Francisco Municipal Railway for the San Francisco Municipal Transportation Agency and covers the area from Ocean Beach and San Francisco Zoo in the west, to Fourth Street and Sunnydale in the east. BART is short for *B*ay *A*rea *R*apid *T*ransport and covers a wider area than the Muni Metro. It is an underground railway system that goes under the bay so that you can get to Oakland on it.

While we were studying the maps in the station, we were approached by a guy offering to help us. I caught on quickly that he was going to want a tip or a hand out, but went along with it. When we told him we had been waiting for a cable car and had given up, he told us that he knew how to get on the cable car without waiting in the queue at the turnaround. He took us back to the turnaround and then walked one block up Powell Street to the next stop. He was a friendly sort of guy and we chatted about San Francisco and London. It appears that he spent some time in London some years before and his summary of the experience boiled down to "I hate your warm

British beer!" As expected he asked for a handout and I gave him $5 which he seemed more than happy with. Within two or three minutes a cable car with a couple of spare seats arrived and we got on.

San Francisco is famous for its cable cars and everyone who goes to San Francisco wants to travel on one. It's an amazing system. Each route has one endless cable running underground and this is constantly moving, driven from a central location. To move off, the car has a mechanism extending through a slot in the street and ending in a gripping mechanism that grips the moving cable, thus pulling the car along. The grip is released at stops so that the car can stop to allow passengers to embark or disembark.

Anyone who has seen the car chase in the film Bullitt knows that San Francisco has a multitude of steep hills and for this reason, all cable cars have three separate brakes! Each car is manned by a two man crew, a gripman (driver) and a conductor who assists with braking and collects fares. There are three routes - Powell-Hyde, Powell-Mason and California Street. All cars have open sides with people standing on the 'running boards' along each side of the car when the inside is full. The bells the cars use to advertise their presence at intersections provides a constant backdrop to the soundscape of San Francisco.

Fisherman's Wharf is at the north east corner of San Francisco and was originally a wharf for the local fishermen. Now it is a tourist trap of the worst sort, so bad in fact that it has to be visited just to see how appalling it is! The views across the bay and of the waterfront piers are stunning, however the commercialism behind the waterfront takes some believing with shops and shops full of tourist tat. The highlight of the day for us was catching a beer outside a bar in the Cannery, one of four malls in Fisherman's Wharf, where there was a live blues player playing San Francisco Bay Blues. His name was Dave Earl and Adam and I really got into his music, so much so that I bought his CD when he finished his set.

We also took the chance to grab some lunch and had some clam chowder in a hollowed-out loaf, again the touristy option, but I have a fondness for clam chowder and it was good chowder despite its origins. Along the waterfront there are several stores selling shrimp and crab but rumour has it that these are flown in from Canada and not locally caught. I expect the chowder arrived in a tin from some place far away from San Francisco, but we enjoyed it nonetheless.

The Powell-Hyde line turnaround had long queues and we therefore tried the trick of walking up to the next stop. However this time we had to wait for three cars to go by before finding one with a couple of spare seats. We got off the cable car at Chinatown so that we could walk through it to the Financial District and catch the bus back to the RV Park.

Chinatown was delightful. There is a Chinatown area in London, but the one in San Francisco is much larger and seems be more authentically Chinese to me (though I've never been to China!). Conversations were conducted in Chinese and shop signs were in Chinese. The shops themselves sold an amazing array of Chinese goods, from silk clothes, to food, to Chinese cookware and traditional herbs for Chinese medicine – it was all there!

During our walk in Chinatown, we came across a Chinese lady haranguing a crowd from a soap box on a street corner. She was holding a big banner which read:

"BUSH + BLAIR = TERRORISM"
"200,000 DEAD"

It appears Adam and I were not the only people with similar views! I wished that I had taken a picture.

As Adam wanted a Play Station Portable and since we had some time to spare before the shuttle bus arrived, we went looking for one and ended up back at the Virgin Megastore. The Play Station Portables turned out to be more or less the same price as in the UK so we didn't buy one (in fact Adam didn't buy one when we got back to the UK either). Adam however did see another T-Shirt that he liked, and while we were queuing to pay for it, I saw a CD copy of the Easy Rider film soundtrack.

When I was seventeen I had a good mate, Arthur, who was killed in a motorcycle crash. After his funeral I was given the LP version of the Easy Rider soundtrack as a memento and managed to promptly break it whilst carrying it strapped to the back of my bike. I was devastated as it was the only thing I had to remind me of my lost mate and I had ruined it! I had spent the intervening years looking for a replacement off and on and had never found one, until I saw this one on the other side of the world. It's still a great album (and film) - do try and listen to it or, even better, see it. I bought the CD and the same lady served us and she remembered us from the morning.

After a quick coffee we caught the shuttle bus back to Candlestick Park to cook supper. I can't remember what we had, but I do remember that my cough was starting to reappear and that I was getting shivery and starting to ache.

Perhaps I should take this opportunity to say something about the city we had enjoyed so much.

The earliest evidence of a settlement in the area now known as San Francisco dates back to around 1000 BC when there were small hunter-gatherer settlements of the Ohlone tribe around the bay. In the late 1700s the Spanish established a small colony there to take advantage of the natural harbour provided by the bay. The city didn't really take off though until the Gold Rush in the mid 1800's. Initially the San Franciscans headed east to work the claims, but soon realised that there was more money to be made supplying the prospectors travelling from the port of San Francisco to the claims 120 miles east. At the same time Chinese immigrants began arriving, and settling, in San Francisco. These settled immigrants provided the basis of the modern day area of San Francisco now known as Chinatown.

In 1906 there was a massive earthquake, estimated to be 8.3 on the Richter scale, which destroyed vast areas of the city. Even greater damage was caused by the ensuing fires caused by broken gas mains. The fire department was unable to fight these fires effectively as the earthquake had also broken the water mains. The fires were finally stopped from spreading by creating fire breaks, but the area within was totally destroyed.

San Francisco's two major bridges were completed in 1936 (Bay Bridge) and 1937 (Golden Gate Bridge). In the 1960s the area around Haight-Ashbury became a hippy hang-out and drugs were a prevalent part of the 'scene'. To this day there is a hill in Golden Gate Park, near the Haight-Ashbury entrance, known as 'Hippy Hill'.

Today San Francisco is a city of diverse cultures and ethnicities, with a population of around three quarters of a million people. There is a large gay community that can trace its roots back the Second World War and also a large homeless population. Each community is centred on a particular section of the city – the so-called neighbourhoods such as Chinatown.

The architecture is typical of US cities, but there is an open feel to the city that I find attractive. The views from the top of the hills (there are 43 in the city) can be visually stunning, whether over the Bay or over the city. The hills can be rather steep so, unless you are fit and enjoy hill walking, I would recommend using taxis or public transport! Lombard Street in the North Beach area is known (incorrectly I believe) as the world's most crooked street and has eight hairpin bends in one block to facilitate a descent down a hill too steep to be traversed directly. San Francisco is renowned worldwide for its eccentric people; all I can say is that, in my experience, the town has friendly people and a happy 'vibe' to it.

We'd had warm weather and a warm welcome - however the 'cold rain' was still waiting for us!

Chapter 5: (Almost) On the Road Again
(With apologies to Canned Heat)

We had originally planned to head over to Yosemite after seeing San Francisco, but as I was feeling so chesty I suggested to Adam that we reverse the order of our trip and head for Los Angeles, coming back via Yosemite, as it didn't make sense to go hiking in the mountains with a dodgy chest.

I didn't realise at the time what a difference this would make to our trip! Blindly heading for the unknown we set off for Los Angeles, a journey of nearly four hundred miles. Before we had travelled four hundred yards I was deluged by water. The leak had not gone away and there was obviously a chamber or hollow somewhere where the rain had pooled whilst we were parked in San Francisco and it was simply waiting for me to drive off so that it could drip down my neck! That was it. It was time to head back to El Monte as by now we knew the way!

A technician was assigned to have a look at the leak and he pronounced that the 'retro fit' had not been done correctly as it had been done with mastic instead of putty tape. He 'putty-taped' about half of the seam and declared "That shouldn't leak!" By the time the seam was fixed to the technician's satisfaction, I thought that it was too late to head for Los Angeles, especially as I was starting to shiver and ache again.

We had been given a photocopied route to the nearest RV park when we collected the RV and decided to head there for the night and make an early start on our aborted journey to Los Angeles the next day.

As we left I noticed another industrial unit on the trading estate that was the headquarters of Arlen Ness Motorcycles. Arlen Ness is a world- renowned builder of custom motorcycles and although I'm more of a sports \ sports tourer sort of guy, I do admire Arlen's work as he gets more involved in the engineering of his bikes than most of the other custom builders who focus more on the aesthetics. We just had to stop and have a look!

The downstairs part of the large shop was given over to bike and accessory sales, but the upper mezzanine contained Arlen's 'museum'. I was most taken with his double overhead-cam engined bikes. If you're not of a technical bent, you may want to skip the rest of this paragraph! Harley's have a V twin-engine where the valves are operated by push rods. Arlen had fabricated new cylinder heads and crankcases to adapt the engine so as to utilise overhead cams. This is quite a substantial engineering undertaking, and it is this sort of work that gains my admiration.

Adam and I bought the obligatory T-Shirt and headed back to the RV. As we left I saw Arlen chatting to customers, but didn't want to interrupt him, so kept going. It wasn't far to Del Valle (yes I have spelt it right, there's no 'Y') - our chosen RV park. Del Valle is near to the town of Livermore, home to the Lawrence Livermore National Laboratory. This is one of two centres in the US dedicated to the development of nuclear weapons, and houses some of the world's most powerful computers including Blue Gene/L, the most powerful computer in the world in 2005. Livermore is also a wine production centre and is surrounded by vineyards.

Altamont Speedway is also within the postcode area of Livermore and this is the place that the Rolling Stones had their concert in 1969, where a member of the audience was bludgeoned to death by the Hells Angels security (sic). Three other people died at Altamont; two of them died when they were run over whilst sleeping on the ground and the other one drowned. The concert came to be known as "The Day the 60s Died" in later years.

The Livermore \ Altamont area is also known for the number of wind turbines that are situated in the Altamont Pass Wind Farm there. Sources cite over 4000 and they can be seen lining the sides of the road for miles when driving down Highway 580. It was on the Altamont Pass near these wind turbines that we had a minor disaster one year later.

After the usual missed turns and arguments we found the Del Valle camp-site. It's this kind of serendipity that convinces me that travelling to a strict timetable and bemoaning troubles along the way is not only a waste of time, but counter-productive. The joys of travelling for me are in discovering 'little gems' off the beaten track that have not, as yet, been spoiled by tourism. Del Valle was just such a place.

I know that tourism is a vital part of any economy, but please spare me from too many Fishermen's Wharves! Del Valle was delightful. The camp-site was part of the Del Valle Regional Park which is centred on a five mile long lake surrounded by over 4000 acres of unspoilt countryside with beautiful rolling hills surrounding it. As it was the start of the season, there was only one other occupied pitch on the camp-site. The facilities were basic for an American camp-site as they did not include electric hook-up, but we had the battery and a generator to provide mains voltage to charge the battery if necessary, so we were quite happy.

Del Valle

The camp-site was very much in keeping with the surroundings, being well spaced out and with trees to break up the camping field. It reminded me very much of our favourite camp-sites in the UK - the Forestry Commission sites. Both the Forestry Commission sites and Del Valle are constructed to blend in and be part of the landscape, without overwhelming it with man-made precision. We saw countless squirrels which we dubbed ground squirrels as we never saw them climb the trees and they lived in holes in the ground.

Shortly after arriving we went for a short walk and saw a large herd of goats and turkeys wandering over the empty pitches and eagles flying over our heads. The goats were very cute, resting their front hooves on the trunks of trees to enable them to graze on the low hanging leaves. When we arrived at the lake shore we found a bunch of guys with a boogie board being pulled along by a lawnmower engine mounted on a wheeled cart. The cart was placed near the water and the boogie board was then pulled along the shoreline. They were jumping over a stump in the water and videoing themselves doing it. I chatted with them for a short while and they told me that they were hoping to sell the film. They didn't seem overly friendly, perhaps because I had a video camera with me and they thought that I may have been a 'spy in the camp!' A truly memorable walk!

Adam recorded his impressions of Del Valle in his journal, and I would like to share his thoughts with you:

"It was out in the Californian countryside amongst the hills, and every view was breathtaking. The site was amazing. It seemed to swarm with a species of squirrel which we had never seen in the UK before. They were smaller than UK squirrels, brownish-grey in colour, with short tails. Rather than dwell in trees, they had burrows underground and rarely took to the trees. Therefore we called them ground squirrels."

In the evening Adam and I discussed our plans and decided that we would like to spend some more time at Del Valle. As we were so far from the town, we ate in the RV and sat outside at one of the provided picnic tables to eat. In the UK, it is the norm for open fires to be banned on camp-sites, however in the US most pitches have a fire pit. This is a hole in the ground, usually about a metre across, lined with a circular band of steel which protrudes six inches or so above ground level. Often there is some kind of hinged griddle attached for barbecuing. Adam and I both love camp-fires and this simple addition to pitch facilities is a great idea. I wish we could adopt the practice in the UK, but suspect that it is the insurance companies that prevent it from being so. For this reason I find it amazing that it is common practice in litigious America - however they also routinely carry firearms!

A typical fire pit

    Needless to say once dusk fell we got a fire going and enjoyed the camaraderie of the camp fire amongst the solitude of the park. The only fly in the ointment that evening was my increasingly annoying cough and general flu-like symptoms. I had trouble sleeping because of the cough and felt guilty that my coughing was keeping Adam awake.

    The following morning we headed for downtown Livermore to get some cash and do some shopping. After completing our chores we went to a coffee shop for a coffee and a doughnut. When I'm travelling I like to stop at local coffee houses, bars and restaurants to 'people-watch' and eavesdrop on their conversations. I'm not interested in the personal stuff ("Do you know what he \ she said to me last night . . ."); it is the more general topics of what is going on in local and national politics, the new building projects that are planned, the economy and immigration, that interest me. The topics that locals chat about in these places can give great insight into the local area and the country in general.

The weather wasn't particularly good, being misty and damp with intermittent rain and drizzle, so we decided to go for a drive in the local hills. A look at the map showed that Mines Road would be a good road to follow. This road followed the other side of the valley from the Del Valle road and was a tortuous route clinging to the side of the valley, with steep drops off to one side. It is about thirty-five miles long and ends in the town of San Antonio. The views were spectacular, even through the mist and rain, and at times Adam was becoming nervous about the sheer drops at the edge of the road. His nervousness wasn't helped by the sight of a burned out car at the bottom of one steep slope.

There were many places where stopping points had been created for people to stop and enjoy the views, so we stopped frequently to allow me to have a good look. It wouldn't have been a good idea for me to spend too much time sightseeing whilst driving around sharp bends next to a sheer drop! The road climbed upwards from Livermore until it began its descent towards San Antonio. Once we reached the valley floor the road ran parallel to the Arroyo Mocho River, which occasionally crossed the road as a ford. Due to the rain the river was in spate and, where there was no white water, it was deep red in colour owing to the red mud in the water.

On reaching the outskirts of San Antonio we turned around and headed back for Del Valle. I was able to see the views a little better from this direction and we were further from the drop. At one point I saw something in the middle of the road where the double yellow lines were painted. I thought I'd seen something there on the way out, but noticed it earlier going this way and was able to stop. On investigation we found a live turtle just sitting in the middle of the road. As over an hour had elapsed between seeing it on the outward journey and seeing it on the return, it must have been sitting there for some time. It's lucky that there's very little traffic on this road or it wouldn't have survived! We took some photos and moved it to a safer location off the road near the river. While we were parked-up, we made some bacon sandwiches in the RV for a late lunch – yet another great spot to eat!

After our impromptu lunch, we continued our journey and saw some guys riding dirt bikes up and down the side of the valley. "Good Luck", I thought! Further down the road we stopped to admire the view and whilst we were there we heard the squealing of tyres and a BMW laden with teenagers came around the bend with its tyres skidding in a controlled four wheel drift. I then understood how the other car that we had seen earlier had come off the road! This was one of about five cars that we saw on the journey, and I think that the lack of traffic made the trip even more enjoyable.

I don't know if there would have been more sightseers on the road if the weather had been clear, but it gave us both a back-to-nature wilderness experience, prompting Adam to comment that it had been "a very spiritual drive".

The lucky turtle on Mines Road

As we had only booked and paid for a single night at Del Valle, we needed to pay for another night. We'd stopped at the Ranger Post on the way out to pay for another night and at first the Ranger had seemed rather curt but became more friendly when we asked about an extra night. I think she thought that we'd stopped to complain about something until we explained we liked the place so much we wanted to stay another day. She advised us to pay when we returned later in the day but when we returned to the Ranger Post, it was closed and there was no-one around.

We headed to the camp-site anyway, fully intending to pay in the morning before we left but as we turned on to the camp-site we saw something labelled 'Iron Ranger'. This was a hollow square metal post set in the ground, about one metre high and had some envelopes in a holder at the top. You selected a vacant pitch and then filled in your details and the pitch number on the form on the outside of the envelope. You then put the necessary fee in the envelope and 'posted' it, keeping the detachable flap of the envelope to display on the pitch as proof of payment. A modern 'honesty box'!

Once we had set up camp, Adam took himself off for a solitary walk around the lake. I wasn't feeling up to a walk and had a bit of a kip in the RV. When Adam returned from his walk, we sat outside the RV and whilst we were there a small herd of three deer wandered past - a lovely sight to see.

The next morning we rose at 6.30 to make an early start on our journey to Los Angeles, planning to stop for breakfast en route. It is far more common to eat breakfast out in America than in the UK and it can often become either a business or social meeting. Before we had covered two miles, Adam was complaining of cold water dripping down his neck. The repair "that shouldn't leak" had merely shifted the problem from one side of the cab to the other! After a substantial American breakfast in Livermore, where I was able to do more people watching, we yet again headed back for El Monte in Dublin.

Having water dripping on your head whilst driving is both uncomfortable and distracting, but not as distracting as negotiating with the Californian emergency services, which I would be doing shortly!

Chapter 6: The Long and Winding Road
(With Apologies to the Beatles)

El Monte decided to replace the RV (I wish that they'd done that the first time!) and we spent about an hour and a half transferring our belongings to the new RV. I'd like to say ALL our belongings but I subsequently found that I'd left our underwear, socks and a video camera charger in a drawer in the old RV!

By 10:15 we were back on the road heading for Los Angeles. As we left Dublin the rain was pouring down, but it soon gave way to bright sunshine. The central plain of California is called the San Joaquin valley and is very flat with considerable arable farming. Crops include grapes (for wine), raisins, citrus fruits, asparagus and nuts (almonds and pistachios). It is estimated that 25%, by value, of America's agricultural production comes from the San Joaquin Valley.

We were travelling down the main arterial route through the valley, the *I-5,* (OK it's not winding, but it is long!) and after 150 miles we stopped for gas, stopping again after another 100 miles for a top up of gas and something to eat. In America there are two types of service areas; a basic 'rest area' provided by the local state with parking and restroom (toilet) facilities and a 'travel plaza' (similar to a British motorway service area, but with more choice) where there is usually gas and a selection of restaurants and shops.

We chose to eat in an 'Iron Skillet' which claims that it "serves professional drivers". The menu was more varied than would usually be found in a UK motorway service station and Adam had a bacon cheeseburger and I had shrimp (prawn) linguine with mushrooms. My linguine came with a bowl of soup and a side salad, but as I was steadily feeling worse and losing my appetite, I declined the soup but did have the side salad from the well stocked salad bar.

Sitting at the next table to us was the largest American we had seen so far tucking into an enormous spread of ribs and fries with many side dishes (America seems to have given the English speaking world a new culinary noun: 'sides' - Ouch!).

Dining out in the US is a little different from the UK. For a start the portions are much bigger than we are used to and salads are served before the main course rather than with it. Coffee usually comes in a 'bottomless cup' which means that when it gets low a waiter or waitress will fill it up at no extra cost. It is usual to tip comparatively generously, usually 15% of the bill, as service wages are low in the US and waiters and waitresses expect to make the bulk of their income from tips. For this reason service is generally good and the staff friendly. If service falls below accepted standards, it is OK to give a little less than the expected 15% - and vice versa! Before leaving the travel plaza I called in at the supermarket and bought some over-the-counter cough syrup, but it didn't help.

At one point in the journey I saw three articulated lorry tractor units being transported. The first was being driven normally and the second had its front wheels linked to the fifth wheel (hitch) of the first, with the third being similarly attached to the second. One driver, three trucks moved!

Shortly after resuming our journey we started to climb into the Tehachapi Mountains and the weather deteriorated dramatically. From bright sunshine we entered fog interspersed with heavy rain, with the rain dominating the higher we got. Feeling ill and tired from the journey, I decided to stop short of Los Angeles and we consulted the RV park guides provided by El Monte. Up to now I've named the RV parks and companies that we used, however I will not do so this time - you'll know why shortly! We chose a camp-site a few miles off the I-5 and when we arrived we very nearly changed our minds as it looked so run down and resembled a shanty town. I decided to stay even though the site was uninspiring as I felt so tired and run down and reasoned it was only for one night anyway.

Despite the beautiful surrounding countryside, the whole site was laid to asphalt and most of the RVs on it looked like wrecks. The prevalence of porches and annexes along with portable car garages gave the impression that most of the residents lived there permanently. Checking in, I totally confused the lady in reception as it was obvious she'd never had to deal with anyone from the overseas before. There was a computerised check-in system and it baulked at UK addresses and telephone numbers. She had to go and find the manager to work out how to check us in. I don't know what he did but he sorted it out quite easily and we were allocated a vacant pitch on the crowded site.

That evening I took a shower and it was then that I first discovered the missing underwear and socks. As all of my clean underwear and socks were missing we had to go and do some laundry. The one good thing I have to say about this site is that it had a good laundry, which bailed us out of a hole. However I still have vivid memories of traipsing backwards and forwards between the laundry and the RV in the pouring rain to check on progress and feed the dryers. If the camp-site itself was depressing, the weather and my degenerating health greatly added to the feeling of moroseness.

We were about 35 miles from Los Angeles and, as it was a weekday, we decided to make a later than normal start in an effort to beat the rush hour traffic. Adam was keen to see Hollywood and visit Little Armenia, an area of Los Angeles near Hollywood that was the birthplace of one of his favourite bands, System of a Down (SOAD).

The trip into Hollywood was quite slow despite leaving after the peak rush hour and we parked the RV on the side of the road on Hollywood Boulevard at the start of the 'walk of fame' where there are gold star emblems set into the pavement with media stars' names attached to them. As we walked along the walk of fame, I realised how tacky and run down the street really was. There were countless sex and lingerie shops and I guess the prevalence of these shops gives some insight as to how some out of work actresses may earn a living!

At one point we went into a booth advertising a free map of Hollywood. It turned out to be a 'come on' as they immediately offered us a bus tour of the 'homes of the famous'. I'm not a star-struck person and so declined, but they did give us the promised free map which identified the location of the pavement stars according to artist name.

The weather was rather wet and I remember slipping around on the pavement because of its polished nature. Adam and I are both fans of Jimi Hendrix's music and wanted to see his 'star' so headed down the street to find it. Along the way I noticed the star for Nelson Eddy, a singer my Mum particularly admires, so we took a picture of the star just for her - I hope that she enjoyed seeing the picture on our return.

As we walked down Hollywood Boulevard, we came across a 'Supply Sergeant' Army Surplus store and spent a happy half hour browsing around looking at the items on display. Adam liked the look of a NATO camouflage jacket and bought it. By this time we were near the limit of the parking meter time and headed back for the RV, stopping en-route to take pictures of the famous Hollywood sign.

From Hollywood Boulevard we headed for Long Beach and eventually found a place to park in a suburban side street. Finding a parking place was complicated by the preparations for the Long Beach Grand Prix which was scheduled for the following weekend. Barriers and grandstands were being erected all over Long Beach and many roads were closed off, making navigation and parking difficult.

After finding a parking spot we headed for the beach and found it to be deserted. It wasn't hard to see why as it was cold and there was a strong wind which whipped up the sand and caused us to be sandblasted for all of the ten minutes we spent on the beach. All rather disappointing for such a beach, and I was glad to get back to the warmth of the RV and get out of the wind and sand-storm.

We had selected Dockweiler RV Park as the place to stay in Los Angeles and made our way there after leaving Long Beach. Dockweiler RV Park is right on the edge of Dockweiler Beach, being separated from the beach only by a low wall. The park itself is all asphalt but is on two levels rising from the beach so most pitches have a great view over the beach.

The park backs on to the Hyperion sewage treatment plant and is just a mile or so from Los Angeles International Airport. Despite the proximity of the plant, we never noticed any unpleasant odours mainly, I think, because the prevailing wind was blowing off the sea. There are palm trees all over the site and, despite the asphalt and sewage treatment plant, it was a picturesque setting to camp in. Not only were the surroundings much better than the previous site, but the nightly rate was less!

We arrived at about 2pm and set about making a late lunch of Bratwurst. After lunch my cough started to get worse than ever and I was beginning to cough up green phlegm. "Enough is enough", I thought and headed for the reception to find the address or telephone number of a local doctor to get some antibiotics.

At reception I enquired how I might contact a local doctor only to be told "You've got a cell (mobile phone) haven't you? Call 911". I explained that I just had a chest infection and needed to get some antibiotics from a doctor and didn't need an ambulance or a trip to hospital, just an appointment with a doctor - tomorrow would do! I was told, firmly, that in the US seeing a doctor was accomplished by dialling 911 and so I did! I asked for an ambulance and was put through to the Fire Department. I apologised for contacting the wrong emergency service and explained I needed an ambulance. The operator told me that the Fire Department ran the ambulance service – 'What was the emergency?' I explained about the chest infection and that all I wanted was to see a doctor and it wasn't an emergency. I even told the operator that I thought it was odd that I had been advised to call 911 as it wasn't an emergency and the UK ambulance service would be mightily upset to come out for a simple chest infection! "The ambulance will be with you shortly" was her reply.

I guess that in America they have to despatch an ambulance once you have called. True to her words the ambulance was there in less than ten minutes, closely followed by a fire engine. As I would have expected their British counterparts to be, they were not amused to be called out for a chest infection. I explained that it wasn't my idea as reception had advised calling 911 despite my protests. The paramedics were extremely sympathetic in the circumstances and gave me a map to the nearest emergency doctor and promised to have a 'word' with reception on their way out. Thanks guys, you were brilliant!

Chapter 7: Lazing on A Sunny Afternoon
(With Apologies to the Kinks)

The map left by the ambulance guys indicated that the nearest emergency medical centre was situated within the grounds of Los Angeles International Airport (LAX). As we entered LAX we could see the hospital where the emergency medical centre was located, but couldn't get to it because of the dual carriageways and one way systems. After covering several miles touring the outskirts of LAX, we managed to turn into the road next to the hospital, only to find that the hospital parking was in an underground garage, with a maximum height restriction lower than the height of the RV.

The hospital was located next to a police station and I turned in there and found a parking spot but was concerned that I'd end up being clamped or fined for parking where I wasn't supposed to. As I sat there agonising over what to do, a police car turned into the car park. I went over to him and explained the situation asking if it would be OK to park – fortunately he said 'Yes'.

We went into the emergency medical centre where I was asked to complete several forms and then asked to wait. I was glad to see that the waiting room was quite empty, expecting that it wouldn't be long before I was seen. As we waited, people were periodically called and disappeared into the treatment area while others arrived, completed the paperwork and sat down to wait.

Time passed and I noticed that people who had arrived after me were being called so I went to the reception to ask when it would be my turn. They checked their records and then started arguing amongst themselves about a signature on my form. Evidently this signature indicated that I had already been seen, and they were trying to establish who had put it there erroneously. I didn't care! I just wanted to get in and see a doctor!

Ten minutes later I was led into a treatment room that was already occupied by a very surprised half-dressed lady. The medical orderly apologised and led me to another treatment room, took my history, and did the basic medical checks such as temperature and blood pressure. The doctor arrived fifty minutes later and spent all of two minutes diagnosing 'acute bronchitis' and then prescribing an antibiotic. On my way out I had to pay two bills, $50 for the hospital and $75 for the doctor. I make that about $37.50 per minute, or $2250 per hour, for the doctor! Nice work if you can get it.

We were then directed to the nearest pharmacy but by this time it was dark and we had difficulty finding it. Eventually we did and I got my prescription filled out (another $44). My travel insurance refunded all of my medical expenses (less my excess) and it was a great comfort to know that I needn't worry about the cost of the medical treatment.

When travelling outside of the EC, travel insurance is a MUST and it's also advisable to insure within the EC as well, as it covers emergencies other than just medical, such as breakdown, vehicle recovery, trip cancellation and lost luggage. If you're planning to undertake any hazardous sports or pastimes you should tell the insurance company - or you may not be covered! I told my travel insurance company that I intended hiking and wild camping in Yosemite and that I would be riding a motorcycle. They added nothing for the hiking and camping, but added around £2 for the motorcycle riding. Most travel insurance companies cover riding motorcycles up to 50ccs, but after that will add a small premium. Had I had the misfortune to fall from the bike that I hired, my medical expenses would have been covered but, if I hadn't told them, it would have necessitated 'open wallet surgery'!

The journey back to the camp-site will stay in my memory for a long time. We got hopelessly lost and this resulted in the classic driver/passenger argument: -

Driver: "Which way now?"

Passenger (looking at map with panicked expression): "I don't know... Oh! I think we should have taken a left back there!"

Most of the roads were dual carriageways, so turning around was difficult and after half an hour or so of chasing our own tailpipe, I finally gave in and stopped at an all night garage to ask directions - and so exhausted, we finally pulled into the RV park.

After returning from the hospital Adam was feeling restless and took a stroll on the dark beach. His journal records "*I was feeling kinda depressed, so I listened to the waves and drew stuff on the sand. It really helped. The moon was crescent and Orion was clear."*

I didn't sleep too well that night due to incessant coughing, and must have also kept Adam awake, but I finally managed to doze off.

We had a slow start to the next day and ate a lazy breakfast of basil and garlic sausage sandwiches. Despite liking basil and garlic (and sausages!), I didn't enjoy them too much. I felt a little better shortly after taking the next dose of antibiotic and some pain killers and we went to do some shopping. We stopped off at reception to book another couple of nights as I wanted to take it easy for a while to allow the medicine time to work. We also arranged to change pitches as the one we were on had an overflowing septic tank.

The previous day's weather had been a little miserable but now it was glorious, with bright blue skies and brilliant sunshine, giving rise to sun kissed views over a glittering ocean.

For ease and simplicity we had tinned stew for lunch. I thought that it was OK to fill a hole but, Adam was more forthright saying "I don't like it". After lunch Adam suggested that I had a lie down while he washed and dried the dishes (Bless him, he didn't realise quite how much I appreciated his kind offer!). Whilst I was napping Adam went for a walk on the beach and took some photographs which turned out to be very good.

I was concerned that Adam would be bored by our enforced idleness. However he took it very well and even seemed to enjoy it - he noted:

"Today we didn't go anywhere but I enjoyed it more than days when we did go places. This morning we went to a 7- Eleven for supplies, changed our pitch on the RV park and booked two more nights here in L.A. Weather was amazing, my arms are bronze. When walking on the beach this morning I found a ball which I have been bouncing around the site. I skimmed stones along the waves and combed the beach for shells. I took a truckload of photographs, some of which I'm proud of. In a lot of ways having a day of relaxation was good - for instance I got to talk to my Dad about stuff.

I enjoyed it. Sunset today was beautiful and, having never seen palm trees before, I took pictures of both."

Sunset through the RV windscreen on Dockweiler Beach

I had taken the next instalment of pills with lunch and, after my rest, was starting to feel a lot better. Adam and I took a short beach walk where I took some photos and enjoyed both the sunshine and the peaceful beach. Despite the sunshine there were very few people on the beach and they were mostly cycling, walking or roller-blading along the asphalt path near the higher edge of the beach. It is not unusual in the US to have a path along the upper edge of the beach. Sometimes it is paved in some way, and on others (such as Daytona Beach in Florida) it is just compacted sand which people can drive on. To Adam and I it seemed strange to see this constant traffic along the edge of the beach as we were more used to UK beaches where this does not happen.

There were only two or three groups actually sunning themselves on the sand. Sitting in the RV taking it easy and watching the world go by for a while made me realise how seriously Americans take beach safety. There are lifeguard towers every few hundred yards and you are not allowed to take alcohol onto most beaches. Also, despite the scarcity of people on the beach, two different agencies regularly patrolled the beach in 4 x 4s (Life Guards and another group which I can't remember). In addition to this I saw a US Coast Guard helicopter flying along at about 100 feet above the surf line every hour or so - even though we were only a mile from the end of LAX's main runway!

It also occurred to me that many Americans wear the type of uniforms that we in the UK would associate with the police or military, even though the posts that they hold are not connected in any way with the police or military. Security Guards, Park Rangers, Concierges, Tour Guides and even the Emergency Medical Technician (EMT: UK, Nurse) had military-style uniforms. Perhaps it is indicative of America's attitude to authority?

As we had a little more time to spare, I decided to make a chicken casserole and spent some time preparing and cooking it; all told it probably took about three hours to prepare and cook (though I didn't need to be constantly standing over it). With the facilities available in American RVs it is possible to cook quite elaborate meals, the only limiting factor being space for serving and preparation. The small sink and draining board also hamper the washing up. For anything complicated you need to be disciplined and neat. A one pot meal like a chicken casserole (I put the potatoes in with the rest of the casserole near the end of the cooking time) is ideal. No need to juggle pots, pans and plates when serving, and only one pot and two plates to wash up.

During an eight-day power failure following the storms of October 1987, Simone and I cooked our way through the contents of our freezer in a similar kitchen in our caravan. Our home cooker had a gas hob and an electric oven, so for anything that required oven cooking, such as roasts, we had to resort to the caravan oven. In those dark days (no electric lighting) we had several dinner parties for neighbours who only had electric cookers so we were able to cook both our and their food before it spoiled as we needed to 'use it or lose it'. It became a regular occurrence for Simone, Adam or myself to bake a cake when we are on holiday in our caravan. Cooking excellent meals in such confined spaces is possible providing you plan beforehand and clear as you go. Did I mention that I'm a foodie?

Adam doesn't like washing up (who does?) and we had developed a system where whoever didn't cook had to wash up. On this occasion I cooked and he washed up, but he was probably cooking more meals than I did. I didn't mind because I think that cooking is a basic life skill that everyone should master to a greater or lesser extent and this was an opportunity for him to learn. Following these beginnings he has turned into a very capable cook and cooks frequently. We have a dishwasher at home so the cooking / washing up rule doesn't apply there!

After clearing up the supper things we got talking and shared a few beers with the guy in the camper across the street. His name was Bart and he was a set painter in Hollywood. His home was in Alaska and he divided his time between Alaska and Hollywood, coming south when he needed to earn more money and living in an old RV whilst he did so. Due to regulations concerning lengths of stay on the RV park (and I think other parks in LA as well), he had to move on in 20 days time although he still had five months work on the sets of the TV series he was working on (I forget which one), so would need to find another site. We mentioned our plans to hire a Harley the following day and he suggested that we ride the Pacific Coast Highway, stopping for a while at Venice Beach just north of Los Angeles, as this was where a lot of strange stuff happened, such as people juggling chainsaws.

Today we associate Los Angeles with the movie industry but that is a relatively modern development in the history of the area. The earliest evidence of human habitation in the Los Angeles area dates back to approximately 11,000 B.C and consists of archaeological finds of human remains. The early inhabitants of the area were members of one of the seven native American tribes that made the area their home. It would appear that there was a peaceful co-existence between these tribes and trade between them was commonplace. In 1542 the first European, a Spanish explorer, arrived in Southern California. A little over 200 years later, in the mid 1700's, Spanish missionaries arrived to set up Catholic missions. The name Los Angeles derives from the name of a mission established there in 1781 called '*El Pueblo de Nuestra Señora Reina de los Ángeles sobre El Rio Porciuncula'* which translates as '*The Town of Our Lady Queen of the Angels on the Porciuncula River'*. This subsequently became Los Angeles (The Angels).

For the next 100 years or so some locals embraced the new religion, whilst others fought against it. Mexico declared itself a republic in 1821 and ordered all Spanish priests out of California and land was handed over to friends and family of the new Mexican government. By 1846 the United States had decided to go to war with Mexico and take back land that they had lost. Initially the Mexican forces were able to hold off the Americans, but in 1847 America triumphed and took back California. In 1849 gold was discovered at Sutter's Mill in Coloma, just west of Sacramento and the Gold Rush began. By 1850 Los Angeles had become a city with a population a little over 1,500. The main commerce of the town at the time was the supply of food to the prospectors and miners in the north of the state. The frontier society of the new town of Los Angeles soon gave rise to lawlessness, where law, such as it was, was decided at the point of a gun and violent death was commonplace.

Chinese immigrants came in great numbers to help build the railroads, irrigation systems and, of course, prospect for gold. After the Gold Rush these immigrants sought other work and established agriculture businesses that were now possible because of the improved irrigation systems that they had helped to build.

The main crop was oranges and the introduction of refrigerated cargo wagons on the new Southern Pacific Rail road enabled them to sell their produce nationwide. This produce, with their labels showing the sunny climate of California, attracted yet more immigrants to Los Angeles seeking a life in the sun, despite the lack of any local industry bar agriculture. This lack of local industry changed with the discovery of oil which, for a while, became a major industry, buoyed up by the arrival of the car in the early 1900s.

Until the arrival of the car, Los Angeles had an efficient public transportation system. As car use increased and the auto-mobile industry grew more powerful, the public transport companies began to be taken-over by them and they raised prices to strangle competition with their core business - car production! This eventually signalled the demise of public transportation in Los Angeles and it is only recently that this has started to be addressed and a new public transport infrastructure introduced.

In 1914, Cecil B. DeMille, Jesse Lasky, Sam Goldwyn and Arthur Friend shot the first full length feature film to be made in Hollywood. From this beginning the movie industry boomed in Los Angeles and is now, deservedly, the world famous centre of the movie industry. Alongside the movie industry, the aviation industry grew, with many factories, airfields and military test ranges being established. The China Lake Naval Air Weapons Station, where air weapons systems are designed and tested, is 150 miles north-east of Los Angles, and was established over 50 years ago. We would pass this enormous military station later in our trip.

Hollywood's nickname is 'Tinseltown' and I think this is a very descriptive epithet. Tinsel is flash, decorative, gaudy, superficial and without depth. My impressions of Hollywood and Los Angeles are summed up in the same way. The climate is wonderfully clear, the views in the surrounding countryside stunning, the palm trees are exotic, the architecture interesting and the people superficially friendly; however there is a 'tackiness' and 'shallowness' to the whole area which I did not take to. Everything seems to be over-hyped and appearances seem to count more than substance. I may be influenced in my views by the fact that I was ill for most of my time in Los Angeles - but I just didn't like it! I would not have wanted to miss visiting Los Angeles as it is a place that we have all heard about and I wanted to see it for myself, but I won't be in a hurry to go back! For some people it may be the centre of their universe, but it's just not for me.

I was feeling much better from my rest and medication and was now ready for the following day, which turned out to be, arguably the best day of the trip as far as I was concerned.

Chapter 8: Born to be Wild
(With Apologies to Steppenwolf)

I had the first good night's sleep of the trip now that my cough was getting better and I woke feeling better than I had done since we arrived. As we were planning to go to Eagle Rider, the Harley rental shop in LA, to rent a motorcycle for the day we elected to have a late start to let the traffic die down and had a lie in followed by a simple breakfast of toast and coffee whilst admiring the view through the RV windscreen. Looking out over the ocean it was easy to see why the movie industry gravitated to LA. The air is clear whilst the light is soft and unbelievably good with little colour cast, even on a cloudless day. It is perfect for photography or filming, especially at dawn, as we were seeing it, or at dusk - the two 'golden hours'.

The trip to Eagle Rider turned out to be surprisingly short, only about three miles, and we were soon there. I hadn't booked, but had checked beforehand that they had sufficient space for me to park the RV for the day. The guys in the shop were very knowledgeable, helpful and friendly, and we spent some time discussing which Harley would be best for us to hire. We finally decided on a 1500 cc Heritage Softail Classic® because it had a decent pillion seat and a backrest so that Adam, who wasn't used to travelling on motorcycles, wouldn't fall off the back when we accelerated. At the time I would have preferred a Sportster® but they didn't have any with pillion seats, and an Electra Glide® would have been overkill.

The following year when I did hire a Sportster® I discovered that I had made a good choice in the Heritage Softail Classic® as I found the Sportster® to be slow and uncomfortable. The manager at Eagle Rider impressed me with his knowledge of motorcycling as he pointed out the differences I would find between a Harley and the bikes I was used to riding in Europe.

Time again for the blokey, techy, 'boys toys' bit. If this doesn't interest you then I suggest that you skip the next six paragraphs!

By far the most popular motorcycle in America is the US-built Harley Davidson, whereas in Europe the four major Japanese manufacturers are more popular, with Honda the market leader followed by the other three, Yamaha, Suzuki and Kawasaki. Harley's target market is the cruiser as they are built more for comfort and travelling long distances than speed. The emphasis is on comfort and looks as opposed to outright speed and performance. Engines are not generally highly stressed and suspensions are designed for softness and comfort rather than taut handling.

In contrast, the most popular products in Europe from the big four Japanese companies are sports bikes, where engine tuning and performance coupled with race-bred handling are the focus of most riders' attention. To accommodate the different design goals of each type of motorcycle alternative engine designs are used. The Japanese bikes nearly always have transverse four cylinder engines, whereas the Harley machines ALL have in-line V twin engines with a 45° angle between the cylinders. Additionally the Harley engines have valves that are push rod operated, whereas the Japanese machines are universally overhead cam designs.

In basic layout and control functionality the Japanese motorcycles are all very similar, the differences between the marques being quite subtle and confined to minor differences in power outputs, aesthetics and rider 'feel'. However the different target markets and riding styles means that there are differences between Harleys and the Japanese bikes in these areas. On a Japanese bike the ignition switch is normally located on the steering head with the speedometer and rev counter. Touring Harleys such as the Heritage Softail Classic® have the ignition switch and speedometer mounted in the petrol tank (note that there is no rev counter). Additionally the ignition key is removed after starting the bike, unlike the Japanese machines which retain the key in the ignition whilst the engine is running.

Seating positions are radically different with Harleys having a feet forward / backward leaning seating position with wide high handlebars as opposed to the sports bike racing crouch with the footrests' position much further back to throw the rider's weight forward on to low 'clip on' handlebars. Touring Harleys have a 'heel and toe' gear change lever which, as the name suggests, can be operated either by the heel or the toe and the rider's feet rest on foot boards. The Japanese sports bike gear levers can only be operated with the toe as the feet rest on footrests that are not much more than pegs or bars to support the rider's feet.

Each engine design has different characteristics. The Harley engine is a low-revving engine that has a wide spread of torque, which means in practical terms that the engine will pull cleanly from low revs to the maximum permissible revs with an even spread of power and no appreciable power band at any particular rev range. Conversely the Japanese engines need to be revved hard to generate their power and have a noticeable power band at some point in their rev range, producing comparatively little power at low revs.

In construction and operation, the American bike seems considerably more agricultural than its Japanese counterpart, for instance changing gear on a Japanese bike is very smooth and slick, there is no mechanical noise generated by the change in gear, and it requires only a short amount of movement of the lever to change ratios. The Harley gear change generates a loud 'clunk' when the gear lever is moved and the movement required is approximately twice that of the Japanese lever. There is nothing intrinsically wrong with either approach to motorcycle building - it is a matter of 'horses for courses' - however I am naturally much more familiar with the European style of motorcycle than the US counterpart. That said, Eagle Rider in LA only rent Harleys, and when in Rome (or in this case LA)...

After my brief introductory tour of our Harley, we set off for Venice Beach heading north along the Pacific Coast Highway. It was great to be back on a bike again and it didn't take long to get into the swing of it and I started to remember what I enjoyed so much about riding a bike. I'd like to say that I enjoyed the feeling of the wind in my hair, but we were both wearing helmets - and you've seen the pictures of me!

American roads are generally straight with few bends but for me, the fun of motorcycling is in taking bends well and feeling as one with the machine as you sweep around the curve. So the Pacific Coast Highway is a perfect motorcycling road for me, with a variety of bends to challenge the rider, I was enjoying myself immensely!

After arriving at Venice Beach we had a walk along the beach, but there didn't seem to be much going on apart from a couple of school parties exploring the sand. I guess it was a weekday and we were too early, both in the day and in the season. My watch had stopped the day before and I wanted to find somewhere that would change the batteries for me and went looking on the local high street. I soon found a jeweller's shop but they didn't change watch batteries so they directed me to a place further up the street called 'Tom Foolery'.

As my watch battery was being changed, we got chatting with the two guys who ran the place. They were both originally from London and had known each other since they were ten years old. In the early nineties one of them had been backpacking around the world when he met a lady in Venice Beach and stayed. A couple of years later his mate came over from London to visit and got together with his mate's girlfriend's best friend and stayed.

They were both bikers so we talked bikes for a while. When we told them that we were going to be riding the Pacific Coast Highway they recommended that we stop for lunch at a restaurant called 'Neptune's Net' situated just on the county line. The two guys wouldn't take any money for the battery change, which I thought was very nice of them. Thanks guys, both for the battery and the advice. If you read this you'll be pleased to know that we followed your advice and had a great ride and a great lunch.

It was fantastic ride up to Neptune's Net - the road was clear of traffic - and as it followed the coast, there were a succession of long gently-sweeping bends which were ideal for our Harley. The sun was bright and the views over the ocean were a joyous explosion of ever changing reflected flashes of light, all the way to the horizon.

Neptune's Net was exactly as it had been described to us - a restaurant where you could sit outside eating under a canopy and watching the ocean across the road. There were quite a few other bikes there and it was obviously a popular destination for bikers. The speciality was seafood, either cooked or raw (for some of the produce that meant swimming in a tank!), but there was also a comprehensive menu of non-seafood dishes. Adam and I both had bacon cheeseburgers which Adam had developed a taste for whilst we had been in America. They just 'touched the spot'.

After lunch we rode a little further north but the road soon became a regular interstate, i.e. a straight dual carriageway. As this made for boring riding we turned off to explore some minor roads, but they too were straight and were surrounded by fruit fields with gangs of labourers working in them. Getting bored with the straight roads, we turned around to head back to the Pacific Coast Highway. As we approached the main road junction, we saw a display of missiles and aircraft at the side of the road. These were part of the local Navy Base and looked quite spectacular; even a little intimidating!

The ride back was as good as the ride out and the change in direction meant that we had a whole new supply of views to admire. We stopped in Malibu for some petrol and to collect supplies at the local supermarket. Luckily the bike had panniers so we were able to carry the items that we bought without any problem. As we approached Venice, the traffic started to get really heavy as it was the evening rush hour and I was glad that we were on a bike and so were not stuck in the traffic like most of the other drivers who were cooped up in their cars. If we had have been in a car, I suspect that we wouldn't have made it back before the shop closed but we arrived in good time and the staff were as friendly as ever.

The rental documents showed that we had covered 117 miles on the bike. One lady took some pictures of us and the bike (you can see one of them earlier in the book).

Adam's journal entry for the day reads:

"Today was awesome! We rented a Heritage Softail Classic® Harley Davidson for the day. This was the first time that I had ridden on a motorbike for any great distance. The people at the rental place were friendly and helpful - the bike was awesome. Dad was an excellent rider (thanks son!). *We rode north up the Pacific Highway for roughly 60 miles. We stopped at an out of the way restaurant called Neptune's Net - a popular bikers' hangout it seems. . . .We had bacon cheeseburgers and chips which were very good. During the ride we passed through a sort of hill-billy community. There were lots of fields and about twelve people on tractors doing weird hick-stuff. . . Weather was amazing - sea was idyllic - best day of the holiday so far.*

PS I need a motor bike."

We rounded off the day with a meal of home (or should that be RV?) cooked pork chops with mustard, garlic and sage accompanied by filled pasta and sweetcorn - an ideal end to an ideal day. As we sat in the RV that night, Adam said that he would like to see Death Valley as he'd never been to a desert before and very much wanted to go.

We spent some time looking at maps and decided that it would be too far out of our way to go through Death Valley itself, but it would be possible to go to Yosemite via the next valley along, Panamint Valley. Little did we realise at the time what a profound effect the decision to go to Yosemite via Panamint Valley was to have on our trip!

This one day in the saddle prompted me to buy another bike a few months after our return home (a Honda). I still ride regularly, covering around 10,000 miles a year. Adam and I have toured France on the bike and travel to the Isle of Man TT motorcycle races regularly. Adam is only here because Simone and I met through motorcycles when some friends and I saw her 900cc Ducati Darmah (an exotic Italian motorcycle) outside a local pub and went in to see who owned it. We celebrated our twenty fifth wedding anniversary by riding our bike to Brussels for a long romantic weekend. I'm telling you this in the hope that I can convey to you the change that this one day riding a bike in California has made to all of our lives, because then you may get some idea of how much Adam and I enjoyed it.

Chapter 9: Down in the Valley Below
(With Apologies to Led Zeppelin)

An early start! A quick cup of coffee and some toast and we were on the road. The traffic leaving LA was heavy for early on a Saturday morning but not as bad as we had seen it earlier in the week. Adam navigated excellently as we joined the I-5 going north without problems. We turned off onto the R-99 making good progress to Bakersfield. From Bakersfield we took the R-178 towards Ridgecrest although progress on this road was a lot slower. The R-178 goes through the Sequoia National Park and initially follows the banks of the Kern River.

The views were spectacular but there were some worrying sections of the road with sharp bends and sheer drops. On the right hand side of the road, which we were driving on, was a sheer cliff rising from the road edge and when the road had been made, it had obviously been blasted with explosives in places to give the road an easier path around rocky outcrops. This had left pieces of harder rock protruding from the cliff face on the sharper bends. This is not a problem for a car, which would pass below them, but with a large vehicle like an RV, care had to be exercised!

About 40 miles out of Bakersfield we pulled off the main road into the small town of Lake Isabella (named after the nearby lake) to have lunch. We found a small family-run restaurant and had their 'Western Burgers' (bacon cheeseburgers with onion rings), which were obviously home-made burgers and were excellent. Burgers in America are generally much better than those in the UK, and these were the best we had eaten since our arrival. I think they are better as a result of the higher quality meat that they use; in fact the quality of all the meat we had bought in US supermarkets was better than any we would have found in any UK supermarket. The service at the restaurant was good and we got chatting to the waitress about the UK, and Yorkshire in particular, as she had family in the town of Wetherby, close to where a friend of ours lives.

After topping up with fuel, we continued along the R-178 until we got to the junction with the I-395 near Ridgecrest where the road system became quite complicated. However, Adam did a superb job of navigating me through it all and we ended up on a single carriageway road heading for the Panamint Valley, which is within the Death Valley National Park.

To our left was a long chain-link fence which was the boundary of the China Lake Naval Weapons Centre. I couldn't believe how long it was as we must have been driving past it for a good 20 miles (I subsequently found that the base fence encompasses an area of 1.1 million acres) before it started to divert from the road. After leaving the fence behind, we soon saw a sign that said we were about to enter a desert.

Travel was rather slow due to the many bends, but each bend brought a new stunning view and we stopped frequently to take pictures. We saw mountains, some of which had snow on their peaks, valleys, plains and desert. It seemed quite strange to be standing in the baking, dry and sunny desert looking at snow covered peaks! California certainly has a landscape of contrasts. We passed a couple of dry lake beds fringed with white mineral crystals. Further up the road were two towns set very close together, Argus and Trona. Both were very run-down, dry, dusty and depressing. I wouldn't want to live in either as both towns were so small, remote and dusty looking.

After leaving Trona the views, unbelievably, became more spectacular. At one point we stopped in a pull-over where there were some plaques telling the history of a couple of nearby ghost towns - Ballarat and Panamint City.

By this time we had been on the road for about eight hours (less an hour or so for breaks) and it was time to find a place to stop for the night, so Adam had a look at the sites directory provided by El Monte and found one just outside Bishop. Shortly after turning onto the R-190, we stopped for gas at an unattended station and were soon surrounded by about twenty motorcycles. The noise of those twenty Harleys was deafening above the quiet solitude of the desert!

The camp-site was about 40 miles away and shortly after we turned on to US-395, we saw a sign for another site so decided to check it out. It turned out to be an empty and desolate site with no facilities or people there at all. It was free, but we didn't like the desolate, abandoned feel of the place and continued on our way to the site that Adam had chosen.

We arrived at Keough's Hot Springs camp ground at around 6pm and hired a pitch with no problem. There was no mains water as the overnight temperature still dropped below zero and froze the pipes, this didn't worry us as we had water in the on-board water tank. There were hot springs on the site and the entrance to these was included in the price; however we didn't try them as they closed at 7pm and by the time we had set up camp, we wouldn't have had very long in the springs. The outfit next to ours on the site was the most unusual I had seen, either in the US or the UK, in that it was the smallest caravan I had ever seen, possibly the smallest caravan in the world? We got talking to the occupant and he told us that it had a double bed and a TV. The kitchen was in the rear but you needed to be outside to use it.

Before supper we took a walk through and outside of the grounds. I took some photographs and Adam found an obsidian axe-head and a deer antler. It was quiet and tranquil walking around the outside of the site. Where we were walking, on the desert edge, we were in the shadow of the mountains, but their peaks were bathed in a glorious soft light. It was this light that I had hoped to capture in my pictures, but it was one of those times when the images didn't quite match up to the ones in the photographer's mind's eye. After the walk we had steak, pasta and sugar snap peas.

It had been nice to walk around in the peaceful surroundings with Adam and discuss the trip so far, along with our hopes for the rest of the trip. We were both looking forward to seeing Yosemite, the primary goal of our trip and our destination for tomorrow - or so we thought! We speculated on what it would be like, and what we were hoping to do, as we watched hares in the undergrowth coming out as the twilight descended. There was a gentle breeze and it was easy to imagine how it would have been for the old time gold prospectors alone in the wilderness. As we sat on the sand we watched the sun sinking which threw more and more of the mountain peaks into darkness. All too soon it was fully dark and we stumbled our way back to the RV before tumbling into bed exhausted.

The Sierra Nevada Mountains From Keough Springs

Whilst impressive, I found the desert rather monotonous although Adam had different opinions. I guess that he had more time to look at it and if I'd spent as much time looking at it, then we might have become part of it! Later on I'll include his description of the day, where he describes the desert from his viewpoint so that you get a balanced picture. When Adam first mentioned that he would like to see Death Valley, I had thought of just passing along the edge on US-395, but I'm glad that we didn't as we would have missed so much.

One memory of the day, unrelated to the scenery, remains very clear to me and that was seeing a car pull away from the petrol pumps before the hose was removed. The hose broke at the pump end and as the car pulled away it was snaking behind it. I'm not sure how you could do that unless you were trying to run off without paying. Normally you'd go to pay, and if you hadn't put the nozzle back in the holster, the fuel amount wouldn't register at the till so you'd have to return and replace it. However, pre-payment is common in the US, so maybe that was the reason for this bizarre event.

The dry desert wasn't helping my cough at all so we stopped at a Walgreen's (an American pharmacy chain) to get me some cough syrup. I asked for Pholcodine, a generic cough medicine that I use in the UK which I find to be both cheaper and more effective than proprietary preparations, only to be told that it wasn't available without prescription in the US. I ended up buying a proprietary cough syrup, which didn't help much.

It was amazing to think that we had started the day on the coast at Los Angeles. We'd then driven through the valley next to the hottest place on earth (Death Valley) and were now staying on a camp-site sitting over a natural hot spring, within sight of snowy mountain tops – and it was cold enough at night to freeze water pipes! Only my tiredness, and our collective memories, hinted at the distances and varied terrain that we had encountered over the course of the day.

Time to hear what Adam's thoughts about the desert were:

"Today we set off for Yosemite, via Death Valley - we saw lots of desert. We went through about three native reservations. The desert was absolutely beautiful although Dad said it was desolate and featureless but he couldn't have been looking hard enough ('I was driving!'). There are many hills, many different kinds of sand, plants and rocks, mirages, rattlesnakes, eagles, hawks and much more. We went through a small place near Isabella Lake, pretty much the only true lake for miles. In the desert there are all dry salt flats where water used to be and when we stopped, I threw rocks. Lots of people must throw stuff because we found cans, a TV and an exhaust pipe. Some careless so-and-sos had even left a couple of ghost towns lying around the desert. These are called Ballarat and Panamint City and were both mining towns during the gold rush. We passed through two god-forsaken holes called Argus and Trona. Half of their population have moved out and they will probably both be ghost towns soon.

We are staying at Keough Hot Springs which is situated over some hot springs which heat their swimming pool. To hell with that, where's the cold water? This is the COOL season and during the night the temperature drops below freezing.

During the day I noticed that if I was outside for long without a drink, I became disoriented and I felt almost drunk. Even in the height of summer back home, it takes ages to be that dehydrated, although strangely, I don't sweat too much out there. Dad says that it's because the air is so dry that the sweat evaporates immediately, whereas the moist air of the UK summers is already saturate, so no further moisture can be absorbed - so our sweat doesn't evaporate and that makes us wet and sticky.

I really like the desert."

Retiring for the night at Keogh Hot Springs, we never dreamt that the following day would reveal the consequences of our decision to go through Death Valley National Park!

Abandoned TV in the desert. Why spoil such a beautiful wilderness with rubbish?

Chapter 10: Slippin' And Slidin'
(With Apologies to Buddy Holly)

We left Keough Springs before breakfast and headed for Yosemite. Our proposed route was to continue along US-395 and then turn left at Lee Vining onto the Tioga Pass. This would take us over the High Sierras and at the other end we would pick up the SR-120, which would take us down to Yosemite Village, the administrative centre of Yosemite National Park. In Yosemite Village we would be able to get the necessary permits and hire a bear canister, both of which were essential to camp wild in Yosemite.

Early in the journey we stopped off at Jack's Diner, in Baker, for breakfast. Jack's Diner is a small family run diner attached to a bakery and was obviously the local meeting point for breakfast. I enjoyed a very satisfying breakfast of bacon, scrambled eggs, hash browns and toast. Adam went for the cheeseburger and chips again! It's probably worth mentioning that Adam rarely eats burgers in the UK, as he doesn't like them, but he loved the US burgers that we had whilst we were in California, and made a point of ordering them at every opportunity.

After breakfast we headed for the local supermarket, gas station and ATM to stock up on supplies, petrol and money. The views from the supermarket car park were stunning. The view from my local supermarket is a trading estate!

We drove for about 60 miles on the *US-395* before we got to the Tioga Pass turning at Lee Vining. Unfortunately the intersection was festooned with signs saying that the pass was closed due to snow and ice. Passages in the Yosemite guide books started to come to mind, particularly the ones about the Tioga Pass still being closed at Easter due to snow! I had read about it in the UK, but the closure of the Tioga Pass didn't affect our original plans, as we wouldn't have been using it. Our reversal of the route, and incorporation of the Death Valley National Park, meant that it became a critical part of our route and I'd completely forgotten that it was still closed at this time of the year!

A stunning view from a supermarket car park in Bishop!

As we couldn't turn left we continued on the US-395 and when we got into the centre of Lee Vining I stopped at a gas station to ask for advice and topped up. The attendant seemed quite used to stupid Brits not heeding the guide books and advised that we needed to head for Highway 88, about 90 miles further up the 395. There we could take the 88 to get over to the other side of the Sierras. When I looked at the map, I worked out that the closure of the Tioga Pass would mean a 200 mile plus detour for us. The 90 mile trip up the 395 to Minden (in Nevada) was good driving and pain free, with an ever changing panorama of wonderful views, however the 88 was a different story! It was fine at first, but all too soon had me very unnerved!

Shortly after turning off the 395, we stopped for lunch at a restaurant in a winter resort. The menu mainly consisted of sandwiches and omelettes, however they have a daily special and, on this occasion, it was 'Burgundy Beef' (sic). We both decided to go for this as it was hot 'comfort food' and ideal for a cold day. I was very pleasantly surprised at just how good it was, in fact it was probably the best Boeuf Bourguignon I'd ever tasted - very comforting indeed!

There had been snow patches lying on the side of the road since we turned on to the 88 and as we climbed higher, the snow cover increased until only the gritted road was clear of snow. The way that it clung to the branches of the trees in the surrounding forest made me think of Christmas as it looked so festive. At one point we passed a sign informing us that we were at 8000 feet elevation, and shortly afterwards stopped at a 'rest area' to see what actually constituted a rest area in the US (a large car park and a toilet block). The car park there had been cleared of snow leaving large snow banks at the side of the car park that must have been close to 10-feet deep!

As we began our descent it started to snow, lightly at first, but finally very heavily, and the wind was blowing it horizontally across the road. Previously the road had been clear of snow, but now the snow was falling in earnest and it was starting to lie on the road, making it slippery and treacherous. The wipers were on at full speed but were not managing to fully clear the screen and a layer of ice began to form, obscuring my vision. Fortunately, setting the heater to demist on full blast melted the ice, and that allowed me to see more clearly.

At one point I saw a pick-up truck coming the other way, uphill, with the rear end snaking from side to side as the rear wheels were spinning. The driver didn't seem to have any control and crossed onto my side of the road at one point, causing me to wonder how I was going to stop a heavy RV in time to avert an accident whilst travelling down a slippery slope. Fortunately the rear wheels swung the other way and he headed back onto his (or her) side of the road. If I was concerned about stopping my 25-foot RV, the driver of the articulated petrol tanker following me didn't seem concerned about stopping his much heavier vehicle. He was driving very close to the rear of the RV and, I'm sure, wouldn't have been able to stop before hitting me in the event of me stopping quickly (if that had been possible!). As we drove slowly through the snow storm, Adam was videoing the view through the windscreen, and watching it again in the UK always reminds me of how scared I was during that horrible drive through the snow.

After about twenty five miles the snow storm started to abate, the road was no longer covered in snow and driving became easier. When we arrived in Jackson, we turned south onto Highway 49 and after about 15 miles stopped at a camp ground called 'Gold Strike Village' in the town of San Andreas.

The camp ground had an old gold mine entrance located within it (now securely locked!). It was rumoured to be haunted by the ghost of an old miner, Bob Meaner, and had a hand painted notice on the door saying: "Inside, Old Bob Meaner, Born 1875 – Died? Old Bob Meaner had fire in his eye, was strong as an ox and too mean to die..." At the entrance to the camp ground there was a tin shack with a display of old mining tools which made an interesting focal point. The lady who checked us in was friendly and chatty, as were most people we had met. She told us that she and her husband were from the mid-west, but they spent around nine months of the year touring in their RV and in exchange for the pitch at Gold Strike Village worked around the site, checking people in and doing basic maintenance and cleaning. They had been there for several months and were thinking of moving on shortly.

In the evening Adam and I took a walk into the town of San Andreas and were surprised to hear a deafening frogs' chorus coming from the fields alongside the road. We never saw any frogs but we could certainly hear them. I don't know what sort of frogs they were, but I've never heard anything like them in the UK. It was quite eerie to walk down a deserted street with hundreds of frogs giving voice on either side of us! Curious about these frogs, I tried to find out what sort they were on my return to the UK and found that the frogs of the area had been made famous by Mark Twain in his first published work "The Celebrated Jumping Frog of Calaveras County" and the work is celebrated each year in Calaveras with a fair called the "Calaveras County Fair and Frog Jumping Jubilee". I'm still not sure what sort they were as it appears that they could have been any one of the nine local species of frog or toad.

Adam records:

"We are now about two to three hours out of Yosemite. We are staying on an RV park situated on top of an old 19th century mine. I have seen the mine entrance and it is spooky, dark and flooded but it is locked up, so I couldn't get in. . . . Legend has it that one miner

still haunts the place, having been reputedly trapped in a cave-in, but the body was never found. We left the desert on the way here and very soon found ourselves in a blizzard atop a mountain. The snow was up to a metre thick up on the mountain. The lady who runs this site is friendly. Dad taught me the theory of relativity ($E=MC^2$) conceived by Albert Einstein – spooky! America has some beautiful landscapes."

We made an early start for Yosemite, leaving Gold Strike Village at about 7:30 am, and stopped for breakfast in the town of Angels Camp, "Home of the Jumping Frog", about 12 miles south on Highway 49. We also took the opportunity to do some shopping whilst we were there. Highway 49 was pleasant with steep winding mountain curves and I was enjoying the drive and the views. We were headed for Sonora where, shortly afterwards, we were to turn off on to Highway 120 to take us to Yosemite.

As we approached the 120 junction at around 11.00, I started to experience déjà vu as the signs saying "Highway 120 closed due to snow" started to appear. Foiled again! There was only one thing we could do - continue south on the 49 until we reached Mariposa where Highway 140 branched off to Yosemite. By now we were beginning to wonder if we would ever reach our goal and started to worry that Highway 140 would be closed as well!

At Mariposa our first stop was the Yosemite Visitor Information Centre to find out about the roads and ask about camp grounds. It appeared that all roads into Yosemite, bar three, were closed. Of the three open roads, two required the use of snow chains (which we didn't have). The 140 from Mariposa was the only road open that didn't need snow chains. Finally our luck had changed! The guy in the Information Centre was very helpful, not only about the roads, but with the camp grounds and general Yosemite information as well. He was well informed about pitch availability on the 'official' camp grounds (there weren't any!), but kindly rang a privately owned site and, finding they had spaces, gave us directions to it. The site, Indian Flat Camp Ground, was the nearest site to Yosemite on Highway 140. Having organised our route and accommodation, he went on to explain that there was a bus service that would take us from the camp ground into Yosemite Valley and provided us with a package of useful information. There were pamphlets on all aspects of Yosemite from transportation, to maps, to wildlife, to the local newspaper - 'Yosemite Today'. What a helpful guy!

After getting sorted out with routes and accommodation we stopped for some lunch. More burgers! Adam and I had, by now, eaten more burgers in our short time in America than we had in the previous five years in the UK. I suspect that it has something to do with the quality of the burgers (good) and the alternatives available on the menus (poor); whatever it was, it was doing neither of our waistlines any good! After lunch we paid a visit to the Mariposa Museum which had exhibits about the Gold Rush and the local area, including its geology. Adam bought a book on Native Handicrafts and some stone arrowheads; we ended up spending a happy half an hour chatting with the lady in the museum about our trip to Mariposa and Yosemite.

The trip from Mariposa to Indian Flat was about 30 miles and took longer than I expected because of the twisty nature of the road. For about half of the trip, the road ran alongside the Merced River with spectacular views of the river and surrounding countryside; however, I was glad to see the sign for the camp ground when it appeared at last. Indian Flat was situated next to The Cedar Lodge Motel on the side of the valley and was terraced to give level pitches. The reception area was still being built when we arrived and it transpired that the site had recently been bought by new owners who were undertaking refurbishment and improvement.

After setting up the RV, we spent a relaxing afternoon with Adam reading his book on Native Handicrafts that he had bought in the Museum while I read the one about Yosemite that I had bought at the Visitor Centre (Yosemite National Park, A Personal Discovery). It made a nice change from driving. It had been raining for most of the day, sometimes lightly, but mostly heavily. During a break in the heavy rain we took a walk next to the river and I took some photographs. We also had a wander through the Motel and discovered a series of wooden sculptures of local wildlife scattered around the grounds.

Plans for wild camping had to be abandoned due to the delays incurred because of my health and the long diversion around the closed Tioga Pass. This was a disappointment for sure, but we had also gained much from the changes, seeing places that we hadn't known about before leaving England and meeting people that we wouldn't have otherwise, so were not too downhearted.

That evening, after our supper, we pored over the guides that we had brought with us, along with those we had been given in Mariposa, to decide on our plans for the following day. We decided that the best plan was to catch the Yosemite Area Regional Transportation System (YARTS) bus to Yosemite Valley, which stopped outside the Cedar Lodge Motel next to the camp-site, explore the valley before taking the valley floor bus tour in the afternoon, and then catch a YARTS bus back to the camp-site.

Adam's thoughts for the day:

"This morning Dad woke me up. I had some coffee but still felt tired. We had breakfast in Angels Camp and I had French toast, maple syrup, some sweet butter stuff, sausages and eggs. I ate it all. We drove through some countryside and stopped at Mariposa. There we had lunch (double '49er' burgers), got some info on Yosemite and visited the Mariposa Museum. I bought a book and some native American arrow heads there. I plan to haft them when I am home. (The) Scenery was beautiful! Dad has had enough of driving - he has driven so much recently. Staying on an RV park called Indian Flat."

The following day we would achieve part of our original goal by visiting Yosemite.

Chapter 11: The Sky is Crying

(With apologies to Elmore James, Clarence Lewis, and Morris Levy)

My diary for the day starts with the words "What a glorious day! Yosemite Valley must be the most scenic place in the world!" All of our prior expectations about Yosemite were way short of the mark. We had expected our trip to Yosemite to be the highlight of our trip, and were expecting great scenery, but we were not prepared for the splendour that we discovered in such a small area of the world. Yosemite Valley is four square miles in area and Yosemite village only occupies a square mile of that, but from anywhere in these areas, spectacular views of the surrounding craggy rock faces, waterfalls and granite domes are guaranteed. The views simply took our breath away.

The weather had started poorly, with very low cloud and intermittent rain. The sky was crying! When we got to the valley, the clouds were covering the tops of the mountains and severely limiting the views. It was frustrating just being able to glimpse at the lower parts of the crags, domes, waterfalls and mountains, but having to imagine the peaks, tops and summits. As the day progressed the weather improved, the clouds lifted and the sun came out, and by the afternoon we were able to see the views of the valley in all their glory.

We had risen early and headed to the Motel next door for breakfast. It turned out to be an 'all you can eat' buffet for $8.95. We both went back for seconds and Adam discovered a liking for American pancakes with maple syrup, which proved to be a great success. We were charged $7 each for the return fare when we caught the 8:45 bus from the stop outside the motel and stared in wonder at the views that could be seen through the clouds as we progressed alongside the Merced river to our destination in the valley.

The weather we travelled through is what the Scots would call 'mizzle', a combination of mist and rain that slowly seeps inside your waterproofs, making you cold and wet, and confines your view to a few hundred yards or so - it's less than rain but more than fog. Fortunately the clouds and rain cleared as the day progressed and by lunchtime were all but gone.

The journey took about an hour and we got off the bus outside the Yosemite Visitor Centre. There was a video, 'The Spirit of Yosemite', playing in the Centre showing the history of Yosemite. The original inhabitants of Yosemite Valley were the Ahwahneechee tribe, who originally hunted deer with spears, caught trout in the rivers and foraged for nuts, seeds and berries. Approximately 2500 years ago, they swapped their spears for bows and arrows, making hunting more efficient. The valley was not occupied year round as the tribe moved according to the seasons, following the deer up the mountains during the summer months. Archaeological evidence shows that the tribe traded with coastal tribes and the Paiute tribe who inhabited the eastern part of the Sierras.

The first non-native Americans to see the valley were a party of explorers, led by Joseph Walker. They crossed the mountains from Nevada in 1833, struggling with deep snow along the way (as we had done!). They finally made it to the hills above the valley, but records are not clear as to their impressions and thoughts of the valley.

The Gold Rush of 1849 created an influx of people to the surrounding areas and these prospectors were competing with the Ahwahneechee for food from the land and, using their firearms against the Ahwahneechee's bows and arrows, were able to force them from their lands. Despite the superior fire-power against them the Ahwahneechee fought back, raiding local settlements and killing the inhabitants. To defend the white settlements, the Californian government permitted a vigilante group, which was called the 'Mariposa Battalion', to go into Yosemite and attack the natives. After capturing some of the Ahwahneechee, camped at what is now known as Wawona, the Battalion chased the remainder into the Valley, becoming the first whites to set foot there. The Battalion, in a subsequent expedition, captured the Ahwahneechee chief, and the tribe were re-located to the San Joaquin Valley, which did not suit the tribe and many of them died from diseases introduced by the white man.

In the latter half of the 1850s, settlers and tourists began to arrive in the valley and hotels and lodgings were built. Some of the Ahwahneechee tribe had returned to the Valley and were working as guides and woodsmen, while the women made baskets for sale as souvenirs. Until the 1870s, travel to the Valley was difficult and was accomplished on horseback; however, new roads were now laid allowing easier access for tourists.

Shortly before the roads were laid, a tourist by the name of John Muir arrived in the valley for the first time. He was to have a great effect, not only on Yosemite, but on the protection of wildernesses across America. In 1864 Congress established the 'Yosemite Land Grant' whereby the ownership of Yosemite Valley and Mariposa Grove was transferred from federal to state ownership and a guardian of the land was appointed. Following the Yosemite Land Grant, illegal settlers were moved off or forced to formalise their claims to the land in order to protect it.

The grant was a ground breaking move in the protection of the natural wilderness, but it was not enough for John Muir - he wanted further protections. His opportunity to bring pressure to bear on Congress occurred in 1889 when he camped with Underwood Johnson, the editor of 'Century' magazine, in Tuolumne Meadows. Muir talked to Johnson about the ecology and problems of Yosemite and on his return Johnson wrote a series of articles in his magazine and lobbied Congress, advocating greater protection for Yosemite. As a result Congress created the nation's third national park - Yosemite National. This was a major step forward but Muir still wanted more.

Yosemite Valley was still part of the Land Grant, not the National Park and Muir wanted it incorporated into the Park. He was able to press his case personally when the president of the time, Teddy Roosevelt, visited Yosemite and camped with Muir. Following this visit in 1905, the Valley was included within the boundaries of the Park but unfortunately other lands were lost on the periphery as these were deemed to be of commercial importance. The Sierra Club, jointly founded by John Muir in 1892 and still active today, continued to lobby for an increase in the size of the Park but they were ultimately unsuccessful.

Another influential individual in Yosemite's history was the photographer Ansel Adams who spent many years photographing Yosemite (and other National Parks). In 1934 Adams became a director of the Sierra Club and his images of Yosemite have made their rocky crags and views familiar to millions and have attracted many to the area. Adams worked mainly in black and white with a 10" x 8" wooden camera which used glass plates for the film. This camera was heavy and difficult to carry over rough terrain and he would often wait for hours, or even days, for the light to be exactly right before exposing the negative. He was the inventor of the 'zone system' which is a method for photographers to ensure that the negative is properly and correctly exposed, ensuring that the full tonal range of the media used are represented in the final image. Using the zone system Adams was able to produce stunning photographs and is widely regarded as one of the world's greatest, if not THE greatest, landscape photographers.

In recent times the main issue for Yosemite has been the need to balance protection and conservation with tourism and finance. The sheer numbers of visitors to the Valley are affecting the ecology adversely. On the other side of the coin, the interest shown in the area brings in much needed money and fosters a spirit of conservation that spreads beyond Yosemite to all wilderness and remote areas.

In 1980, the National Parks Service released a plan for the future of Yosemite, but little, if any, of the plan was acted upon until 1997 when the Valley was flooded and had to be closed while clearance and reconstruction took place. This hastened the introduction of an updated plan, the effects of which are now beginning to be seen. A free, low-emission bus service has been introduced, which Adam and I used to get around the valley floor, and improvements have been made in the area below Yosemite Falls. Ironically visitor numbers have declined in recent years due to a number of factors, and this is probably for the good, meaning that the pressure on the environment and ecology of the valley is lessened.

After seeing the video we went to book the Valley floor tour, but found that we had just missed the morning tour, but there was another at 2.00 pm. To utilise the intervening time effectively we decided to walk east along the Valley from Yosemite Village through

Curry Village. We were impressed with how sympathetically the developments in the Valley had been carried out. Buildings were, in the main, made from wood and there were plenty of open spaces between them with many standing trees to break up the development. Our walk was very pleasant - the air was fresh and clean, the ambience 'laid back' and restful. Walking between Curry Village and Happy Isles, near the North Pines Camp-site, we came across two Mule Deer just ten yards off the main path - a lovely sight to see for nature lovers and a good indication of how comfortable the local wildlife are with their human neighbours!

This co-existence between wildlife and humans is not always so benign. Bears are indigenous to Yosemite and California in general. In fact the bear is the state symbol of California and appears on the state flag. At one time the bears were encouraged, with food waste being spread around to entice them to come close enough for the tourists to see them and be entertained by them. The results of bringing wild bears and humans into close contact are all too obvious and many people were injured or killed and, unfortunately, the bears were blamed and persecuted until the practice of laying out food for them was banned. The consequences of this practice are still with us, as bears have learned that where there are humans there is food. As a result there are strict regulations as to how food should be stored whilst in the National Park and now injury and death caused by bears is greatly reduced, although there are still incidents of damage to property, usually cars, caused by people leaving food in places where the bears are able to smell it. It is not only food but any perfumed product, such as soap or toothpaste, that can attract bears and they are quite capable of ripping open the steel panels of a car to get at the 'goodies' inside!

Free 'bear boxes' are available at major trail heads and some camp-sites for the storage of food but if you intend to go backpacking, you are required by law to keep food in a bear canister which can either be rented or bought in the valley for a nominal sum. Normally these canisters are stored outside the tent as bears can still smell the food inside them and you don't want a bear coming into your tent to investigate the enticing smell! Nowadays bears have learned that they cannot get at the food in the canisters and so mostly leave them alone. However, when they were first introduced, the bears attempted unsuccessfully to get at the stored food and this gave rise to the nickname for the canisters - 'bear footballs'.

In the area that we saw the deer there were many large rocks in amongst the trees. These rocks typically had a diameter of around twenty to thirty feet and had fallen off the surrounding cliffs as a result of water infiltrating the natural fissures in the rock face and then expanding during the winter freeze, causing the rock to split. Rock falls in Yosemite normally happen in spring when the ice melts and large rocks come tumbling down into the Valley. This is most unfortunate if you happen to be underneath one at the time!

When we got to Happy Isles we walked a short way up the trail to Vernal Falls. It would have been nice to have followed the trail all the way to the falls as it's only a 1.6 mile round trip along an uphill asphalt path (on the way there). However we wanted to get back to catch the 2.00pm Valley Floor Tour and hadn't yet had lunch so we couldn't afford the time so we therefore turned around before reaching the falls and caught one of the free shuttle buses back to Yosemite Village.

When we arrived a few minutes later, we headed for Degnan's Deli and joined the long queue for a hot dog and a meatball sandwich. This delay meant that we were getting near to the departure time for the tour before we were finished eating, and this was compounded by the fact that we were further from the departure point than we had at first thought - however we made it with scant minutes to spare.

It cost $22 each (approximately £13 at the time) and was worth every cent. I'm not normally one for such tours, preferring to find my own way, but with our shortage of time this was the best option and I would advise anyone with minimal time in Yosemite to follow suit, perhaps taking one of the longer tours where time permits. On the way to the tour, we saw a Stellar's Jay in a tree just off the path and I took the opportunity to photograph it.

Stellar's Jay in Yosemite Village

Whilst in Yosemite Village, we visited the Ansel Adams Gallery and looked at the great man's photographs, along with those of others who have, over the years, photographed Yosemite. I suggested to Adam that if he wished to give me a small present to thank me for taking him to California, the hand-made print of Adam's Aspen trees, made from the original negative by his son, would be very acceptable. He politely declined, claiming that he didn't have the $35,000 (£21,200) asking price!

The tour was two hours long and took in most of the Valley Floor finishing at 'Tunnel View'. The guide was knowledgeable and entertaining and there were many stops at suitable photographic vantage points. I'm not even going to describe all of the sights, there just aren't enough superlatives in the vocabulary, and you wouldn't believe me if I did! Just go there and see for yourself - you won't be disappointed! I'll only say that the best view was the last one from Tunnel View. This is near to the traditional viewpoint of Inspiration Point and is where the road to Wawona passes through the rock. There is a car park just before you enter the tunnel and this is where we looked over the whole Valley. I'm told that it is one of the most photographed views in the world and I can understand why. I've included a couple of shots but to really get a feel for it Google 'Tunnel View Photographs'.

After the tour we did a little souvenir shopping to get some presents for Simone before catching the YARTS bus back to Indian Flats.

As we would be unable, in any practical sense, to go out for a final meal on the last night of our trip (as we would be in Del Valle the following night, and therefore not near civilisation) we made this our 'last night of the trip celebratory meal' night and went to the Motel next door for a 'blow out'. I had Dijon Chicken and Adam chose the BBQ chicken. The meal was very 'laid back' and we chatted for a long time, both to each other and the waitress. It was the perfect end to an exciting and stimulating day. When we returned to the RV, we had a little tidying and packing to do so that we could make an early start for Del Valle on the following day, where we would spend our last night in California before returning the RV. At least there was no washing up to be done!

Time, I think, to hear from Adam:

"Today we went to Yosemite. It was BEAUTIFUL (Adam's capitalisation). Many rocks, trees, waterfalls, ponds, streams, brooks, rivers, plains, mountains, hills, flood plains etc. Their building complexes didn't intrude upon, interfere with, or stand out from the surrounding nature. I felt an urge to be a part of it. In one of the shops I saw two pocket books, one by Sun Tzu (a Chinese general) called 'The Art of War' . . . The other book was 'The Art of Peace' written by Morihei Ueshiba (the founder of Aikido) which was translated from the original Japanese. Both are amazing books. I also bought a trinket for Mum."

Yosemite was a fitting highlight to our trip and we realised with sadness that we would be starting the first leg of our journey home the following day.

Chapter 12: I'm Going Home
(With Apologies to Ten Years After)

We rose early, completed the remainder of the tidying and disconnected the utilities (mains, water and sewer hose) before walking down to the Cedar Lodge for their buffet breakfast. We got there a couple of minutes before the advertised opening time of 7am, only to be told that the chef had overslept and that there would be a twenty to thirty minute delay before breakfast was served.

So we decided to get on the road and cover a few miles before stopping somewhere else for our breakfast. We left Indian Flat at about 7.10 and had a clear and pleasant drive through the spectacular scenery of the Merced River valley. Because of the lack of traffic, we made good time to Mariposa and decided to press on to Merced before stopping for some food. We arrived in Merced at about 9.10 and filled up with petrol but, surprisingly, couldn't find anywhere to eat so kept going north on the I99. At about 9.30 we found a 'Jack in the Box' - a chain of fast food restaurants serving burgers and a range of other snack foods. I can't say that I'm a fan of their food, but it was a welcome sight that morning as we were, by then, getting rather hungry!

By 10.30 we had reached Livermore and topped up with petrol again. As Del Valle was one of the few sites that we stayed on in America without mains electricity (I think possibly the only site), we needed to ensure that the generator would work as it needed at least a third of a tank of petrol to run. This is a design feature to ensure that the generator does not run the tank dry, leaving you stranded. As I was connecting the sewer hose, one of the lugs broke off meaning that it would not connect securely and would have leaked (not a pleasant thought!). Fortunately El Monte had provided a spare, so I used that. I guess that it must be a common fault as the plastic lugs looked thin and brittle and a spare sewer hose was the only spare supplied.

We spent the next couple of hours cleaning the RV and packing. The rental company reserve the right to add on a substantial additional cleaning charge if the RV is returned in an 'unacceptable' state of cleanliness and I didn't want to give them any excuse to levy the charge. After the cleaning and packing we went into Livermore to get some cash from the ATM and some more cough syrup for me. Whilst my cough had steadily improved, the shivering had stopped and I no longer had any aches and pains, I was still troubled with a niggling cough that took a long time after my return to the UK to disappear.

After returning to Del Valle I cooked my last meal in America: Pork chops with sage, filled pasta with grated cheese, and cabbage with bacon along with a white wine sauce. After the washing up I had a doze and then we did the last minute clearing up before turning in for an early night in anticipation of an early start on the following day.

In his last diary entry Adam records:

"I'm coming home tomorrow. Today was nice. We spent three hours driving from Indian Flat to Del Valle. I saw many eagles (and) spent a lot of time by the river at Del Valle. It was relaxing, I felt peaceful. Tomorrow I shall be on the plane home. We shall wake up before 7.00am and will arrive in Britain on Friday."

The day of departure dawned early for us. It was the only day of the trip that I'd set my mobile phone alarm. After snoozing the alarm a couple of times, we got up and cleared the rubbish and unused products from the RV. Soap, unopened soft drinks, uneaten fresh food, cleaning fluids and materials and so forth, all went into the rubbish bin. We had a few tins of food left over and we packed those to take back with us. We collected El Monte's bedding and equipment together and emptied the tanks for the last time before packing the hoses away after first washing out the sewer hose. For anyone touring in an American RV, I *strongly* recommend purchasing some disposable plastic gloves for this task!

The trip from Del Valle to Dublin is only about 20 miles and would take us about 40 minutes during the morning rush hour. Having some time to spare, we stopped for breakfast in Livermore at Emil Villa's, the same restaurant we had eaten in 10 days or so before. We were happy to go back as we had enjoyed our first breakfast there immensely, so we had a leisurely breakfast before heading off to return the RV. The RV checked out OK and El Monte waived the $77 excess mileage charge (incurred due to our detour around the Tioga Pass) because of the leak problems we had suffered. During the thirteen days that we had the RV, we covered nearly 1600 miles - a daily average mileage of 124 miles. However the true daily average mileage would be higher due to the days that we weren't travelling.

Part of the service provided by El Monte was a shuttle bus back to the airport and, because they were waiting for other people to return their RVs before the bus left, we had a couple of hours to wait so we spent the time looking around the upmarket motor-homes that were on sale. Motor-homes like these are rarely seen on the roads of the UK mainly, I think, because of their size, cost and petrol consumption. The largest of these motor-homes has a maximum weight of around 10 tons and, as such, would require an HGV licence in the UK! At around 36 feet in length, 12 feet high and 8.5 feet wide they would also be difficult to manoeuvre around the lanes of Great Britain! I would dread to think what the fuel consumption of one of these 8 litre monsters would be!

These mammoth RVs may be big, but they have every facility and comfort that you could possibly want. They all have 'slide outs', which are sections of the side of the RV that can be extended by a few feet out from the RV using electricity or hydraulics to give a greater floor area. Typically these slide outs are where furniture, sofas and such like, are located and this means that the central floor area is then free of furniture, so giving greater room for the occupants. The galleys have ovens, hobs, fridges, freezers, microwaves and two sinks. There are even separate toilets and shower rooms and a fixed, walk-around bed in a separate bedroom at the rear. TVs are of the large screen variety and there are also CCTV screens and cameras installed to aid in reversing. The driver is able to level the RV from the driver's seat using the control unit for the built-in hydraulic rams at each corner of the RV and the dashboard mounted spirit level. Heating and cooling is taken care of by the multiple air conditioning units located on the roof of these 'homes away from home'. Adam and I marvelled at the luxury and automation, even the steps to climb up to the door were automatically operated! We thought that our rental RV was luxurious, but compared to these it was small and underspecified!

We arrived at the airport in plenty of time and had to wait for the British Airways check in desk to open before we could deposit of our luggage. We then had the usual two hour wait for departure and used the time to buy a few overpriced souvenirs and get some lunch.

The flight was like all intercontinental flights - boring and long. I spent an hour or so chatting with an American, who was visiting the UK for the first time, about our respective healthcare systems and giving him some ideas of places to visit whilst he was in the UK. Eventually, jet lagged, we landed at Heathrow and Simone was waiting for us, having got there an hour early to ensure that we were not left hanging around for her! I don't know why jet lag seems worse going from west to east, but it always seems to be. I was very tired on the way home and for the rest of the day as we excitedly told Simone of our time in California and gave her the presents that we had bought.

Our adventure was over and I would be going back to work the following Monday. It was all something of an anticlimax and home life felt rather strange for a few days as there was no driving to do or impressive sights to see but we soon fitted back into our home life and remembered with fondness our escapades in America. Over the next few weeks I produced a CD slide-show of our pictures for distribution to friends and family and we gradually settled back into our normal routine.

Adam and I thought that we'd been on the trip of a lifetime - but we were both wrong!

Chapter 13: Back Home Again
(With Apologies to John Denver)

Whilst Adam and I were in America, Simone had collected her ailing mother from Brighton and brought her back to our house to spend some one to one time with her. During the years leading up to our trip, Simone's mother had begun the slow, distressing slide into dementia and the week Simone spent with her was the last time that they were able to spend a significant amount of meaningful time together where they were both able to conduct, and remember, normal conversations. I'm very glad that they were able to have this private and uninterrupted time together, free from the distractions of normal family life.

Both Adam and I spent the next few weeks boring Simone, and anyone else who was polite enough to listen, with our tales of America. We both felt that we had been privileged to have been able to undertake such a trip and were grateful for the opportunity to visit an area of such natural beauty and meet so many wonderful friendly people. We had seen wonderful landscapes, eaten delightful food and, by speaking with the locals, discovered the real feelings of the US people about their politics and political leaders. Our one regret was that we hadn't managed to accomplish our goal of wild camping in Yosemite. The limited time we had spent there had only served to reinforce our original desire to get away from the crowds on the valley floor and experience the solitude, splendour and majesty of the wilderness that most of Yosemite is comprised of.

However we still had many fond memories of our time in California such as the guitar player in John's Grill, the Hotel Bijou and Dave Earl in San Francisco, the wonderful wildlife and scenery of Del Valle coupled with our drive along Mines Road after our misfortune with a leaking motor-home. There was also the sunshine and bike ride up the Pacific Coast Highway in Los Angeles, the desert in Panamint Valley, the snow of Highway 88 and the wonder of Yosemite. We also remembered the kind people that we had met: the cashier in the Virgin Megastore in San Francisco, the technician at El Monte, the Park Rangers at Del Valle, the ambulance crew,

Eagle Rider staff, Bart and the guys from Tom Foolery in Los Angeles as well as our many neighbours on the various camp-sites, the Park Rangers and tour guides in Yosemite. All had contributed to an experience that most people would consider to be the experience of a lifetime.

We had immersed ourselves in California, interacted with its society and had benefited from the experience. Most holidaymakers travelling with an organised party end up seeing their destination as spectators, voyeuristically observing the 'natives' and their surroundings before departing for the next place on the agenda. We *experienced* California, its roads, traffic, businesses, medical services, food, scenery, institutions and people. This, to me, is much more important than 'ticking the boxes' on an itinerary dreamt up by a travel agent in another country. We didn't get to see everything we'd planned to, but we did see a lot that we never expected to and were enriched by the experience. As Fleetwood Mac said (in another context!) 'Go Your Own Way'.

Adam summed up his views and recollections of the trip as follows:

"My first trip to America was a memorable one. It had changed how I saw American people and the country as a whole. I had found it much more interesting than I thought I would to begin with. Despite the fact the trip was enjoyable there were a few things that let it down. Dad's illness prevented us from carrying out the thing we'd gone to America for in the first place, (visiting Yosemite) and at the time, perhaps because of his illness, he had a very short fuse. Consequently we argued often, which really put a downer on the trip. That isn't to say it wasn't an enjoyable journey, there was a lot I enjoyed.

However my view of American politicians (particularly Republicans) has worsened if anything. Food in America was remarkably good, as was the price of many things. They have good quality meat, particularly beef, and though they complained about 'gas' prices, they are much lower than the price of petrol in British pumps. I can see why people like America, and why it is considered "the land of the free". They seem much more blasé about 'Health and Safety' and 'Political Correctness' than the Labour 'Nanny State' that exists in Britain. Here it seems we are constantly plagued by men in suits rushing around with political cotton wool to stop us hurting ourselves. Little stickers on cigarette packets stating the obvious, ridiculous amounts of speed cameras, which cause EVERYONE grief one way or another, and many more things, are just some of the ways the British are patronised. There is less of this in America. Guns, land and cars are easier to obtain, I suppose because the relatively recent settling of Europeans in America called for self defence and the ability to settle and start communities quickly.

The highlights of the trip were probably San Francisco, because of the city and the food. Memorable too was the Pacific Coast Highway, because of the views and the Harley, and the food. I also enjoyed the food generally, because a lot of it was tasty, and there was a lot of it (Adam is a bit of a foodie too!). The geography of California is amazing, and the people are generally friendly. Pro-Bush sentiment is low. Wildlife is abundant, and there are many interesting media and historical landmarks, for instance the Borax mines of Death Valley, which were worked by Chinese immigrants in ridiculously bad conditions. They had rationed water and had to guide caravans of borax up to the railways, several miles away. The heat of the desert preserves much of the abandoned settlements.

Overall in some ways I prefer America to the UK, but the UK will always seem like my home some way or another."

As a result of our ride up the Pacific Coast Highway, I bought a motorcycle a couple of months after our return and as Adam and I had abandoned Simone to go off to California, we gave her the choice of where we should go for our summer holidays. She chose the Forest of Dean, an area that we had not been to before. We had a relaxing family holiday there and whilst this is a very picturesque area of the UK, Adam and I felt that its scenery didn't match that in California for variety and splendour.

Whilst staying in the Forest, Adam and I undertook an expedition to the Brecon Beacons (an area of Wales famous for military wilderness training) and spent a night wild camping in our tent there.

Sunset over the Brecon Beacons

Whilst we had a great time and enjoyed the freedom of wild camping it made us think of just what we had missed in Yosemite.

The year progressed in the normal fashion - summer came and went, autumn started and Simone and I trudged along on the treadmill called work. Adam went back to school and studied for his GCSEs. Talking to him over the summer months about the trip and his current views on America and their foreign policy showed that he had indeed modified his views as I had hoped. He still abhorred American foreign policy (as I do), but was now able to see that the actions of politicians, even elected politicians, are not necessarily endorsed by the people they represent, and it is wrong to condemn a nation's people because of the policies of their politicians.

As autumn progressed and the weather deteriorated, my mind went back to the glorious sunny days that we had in Los Angeles and the Panamint Valley and I also thought about the wilderness camping that we hadn't done in Yosemite. In a moment of idleness I recalled that it was at about this time in the previous year that I had discovered the British Airways sale and wondered if this was an annual event.

Curiosity got the better of me and I had a look at their website. I still don't know whether it is an annual event, but they did have another sale; it seemed that fate was beckoning to us. Tempted by possibility I obtained RV rental quotes, started looking at my bank account, and made my calculations. All of which were really unnecessary as I'd already decided that we had to go back and finish what we had started. The calculations were just window dressing to justify my decision. I tentatively raised the subject with Simone and she was (as always) supportive, saying that she wanted us to be able to see and do what we had originally wanted to go to California for, and that she hoped that health issues didn't hold us back this time.

I talked it over with Adam, who was all for it (*surprise surprise!*), and we discussed what we wanted to do this second time around. Camping in Yosemite was top of the list, closely followed by another motorcycle hire, this time for a couple of days. We also wanted to spend some more time in San Francisco and Adam was keen to go to Death Valley itself. Plans were laid, bookings were made and the credit card took a beating. The final plan consisted of repeating some things from before and to do and see some things for the first time. We were going to spend three nights in San Francisco, seeing more of the city than last time and staying at the Hotel Bijou again before collecting the RV. Because of the problems we experienced previously with the leaking RV, I got a quote from Cruise America RV Rentals in addition to a quote from El Monte; however it was considerably more expensive than the El Monte quote so we booked with El Monte again, in the belief that lightning doesn't strike twice. I should have known better, having completed a course in statistics at University...

After collecting the RV we would head for Yosemite and spend around three days there, fitting in the wild camping, before heading for Death Valley (not by way of the Tioga Pass!) and from there we would go to Las Vegas in Nevada. Neither of us had a great desire to see Las Vegas, but we could hire a motorcycle there for a couple of days. Whilst on the bike we planned to go through the Mojave National preserve and then, after returning the motorcycle, head back to El Monte via the Pacific Coast Highway and Del Valle.

After booking the hotel I received an e-mail from them telling me that, as I was staying for three nights, I was entitled to use the free

'Golden Gate Greeter' service. This is organised by Joie de Vivre Hotels (who own the Hotel Bijou) and they match local volunteer guides with visitors according to the visitor's interests. The tours are all custom made for the visitor and when you book you are asked what your interests are, and what you would like to see whilst on the tour, so that the 'greeter' whose knowledge and interest best match your own can be selected. When you meet the greeter you jointly decide on where you will go and what you will see. There is also a social networking website aimed at the greeters and their guests to help you plan your visit, or reminisce afterwards - a fantastic service that has now, unfortunately, been discontinued.

My Christmas present that year was a satellite navigation system (sat-nav) for the car. I already had a hand-held GPS device for use when out walking or camping, but the screen was too small for car use, so I wanted something that would avoid the driver / navigator arguments over directions. In the early days of our caravanning in the UK, whilst I was still coming to terms with driving an articulated vehicle, Simone directed me into a cul-de-sac which necessitated an elaborate turn around manoeuvre and instigated a protracted argument! After using it in the UK, and realising the benefits, along with the pitfalls (sending me up a very narrow lane whilst towing the caravan, so that we found foliage protruding from the caravan when we arrived and we forced several horse riders to turn around and find a farm entrance to stand in so that we could pass), I bought an American map card for it so that we wouldn't repeat the problems that we had in Los Angeles after visiting the hospital. It was several weeks later that I realised that the over-cab bed of the RV would prevent the sat-nav from picking up the satellite signals so had to buy an extension antenna as well.

We were now set and raring to go!

Chapter 14: San Franciscan Nights
(With Apologies to Eric Burdon and the Animals)

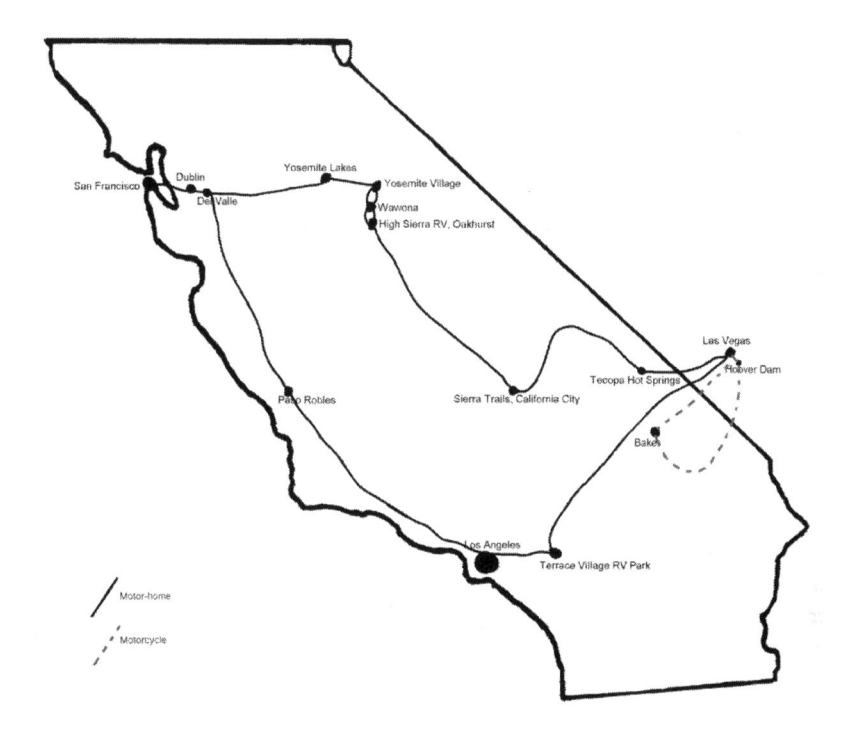

Map of Trip 2

We got to Heathrow at around 7:50, in plenty of time for our 10:50 flight. Simone had dropped us off once again and we struggled into the terminal with our rucksacks and suitcases. The terminal was very busy and we were directed to the longest queue - isn't that always the way? We stood in the queue for about twenty minutes before a BA employee told us that we could check our bags at any desk as we had already checked in via the internet, so we headed for a shorter queue. The check in accepted my rucksack, but not Adam's which had to be deposited at the 'outsize' bag drop. I think this was because I had a cover on mine that stopped the straps flapping around, whereas

Adam's didn't. Once air side we blew £20 on a couple of full English breakfasts and then settled down to wait for departure. Once on board we had to wait for an hour whilst they located, and then offloaded, the bags of a 'no show' passenger. I understand the necessity of doing this, and am glad that they did, as it made my flight more relaxing, however my feelings for the 'no show' passenger(s) were somewhat less charitable!

The flight to San Francisco is approximately 5,400 miles and takes 10.5 long, boring hours by 747. I filled the time by watching the new Bond movie (not as good as the Sean Connery Bond movies - too reliant on gimmicks), eating, drinking and looking at the ground below. Unusually there weren't many clouds and we had a good view of Iceland, Greenland, Canada and North America as we passed over. We overflew many mountain ranges and the views of the sometimes snow-covered mountains were spectacular from above. Whilst over Canada we saw lots of 'grid lines', I don't think that they were roads, but I'm not sure what else they could be. Over the US we saw lots of large, perfect, circles on the ground. As we were at 38,000 feet they must have been huge circles to seem so large to us. I still have no idea how they were made or, for that matter, what they were.

We arrived at San Francisco airport at 14:25 and, knowing where to pick up the shuttle bus, had no problem getting to the Hotel Bijou. When we checked in we were given a complimentary guide book of San Francisco (*San Francisco, Insiders Guide for Urban Adventurers*) because we had booked the stay over the internet. As we had a little time before the shops closed, we just dropped our bag in our room and headed out for some afternoon shopping. As clothes are generally cheaper in the US than in the UK, we'd decided that it would be best to pack light and buy clothes over there, so we got Adam some jeans and trainers and bought some CDs at the Virgin MegaStore, where Adam also bought a Led Zeppelin T-Shirt. Buying the trainers was interesting. I'd found that on our previous trip, some retailers couldn't process my UK Debit Card; some were OK, but others were declined. I guess that it depended on the bank that they were with. It had never been a problem until I tried to pay for the trainers, I just offered another card and the transaction went through. This time it came up 'declined' so I offered another card saying that

I'd experienced this problem before, and that I thought it was down to which bank was processing the transaction. The cashier said that he'd try the card again anyway, and when it was declined again offered his view that it was because my account had less than the $50 asking price in it! As it happened, we were having some building work done at home and I had placed the funds to pay for the first instalment into my account and therefore, at the time, my account had a balance of over £20,000! As expected another card went through without problems, but I felt like telling the store to stick its trainers, and probably would have done if they'd been for me!

After showering and changing we headed off to John's grill again. Despite being rather pricey, we'd enjoyed it last time, it was local and my jet-lagged brain didn't have to cope with difficult decisions on where to eat. Adam had Filet Mignon and I had a New York Strip, both accompanied by baked Idaho potato and a medley of vegetables. Adam doesn't normally like baked potatoes but he enjoyed this one which was served with sour cream and chives. I normally like baked potatoes but not this one as it seemed rather 'watery' and I don't particularly like sour cream! We both had a pud, though I don't remember what it was. Despite my reservations about the potato we both enjoyed the meal, though I wasn't so impressed with the wine. The meal set us back $102, approximately £50 at the prevalent exchange rate, so I don't suppose it was too bad, especially if you factor in the entertainment from the same excellent guitar player, who had been there the year before playing laid-back jazz.

When we got back to the hotel, the helpful receptionist booked us a trip to Alcatraz on the internet. The receptionists were all helpful to the extreme, offering advice on what to do and see, how to get around and so forth as well as booking tickets on-line on your behalf. All in all we had a pleasant evening and meal, despite our jet-lag.

We were in room 207, the room below the one we were in last year (307) and this one was themed on the film 'James and the Giant Peach' and had a framed photograph and description of the film alongside the door.

The jet-lag came back to haunt us at 5 am. As I lay in bed trying to get back to sleep, I remembered that I hadn't called the Golden Gate Greeter to let him know that we'd arrived and make arrangements to meet. By 5.20 we'd given up trying to get back to sleep and headed for the same café as last year to get some breakfast.

Adam seemed quite pleased as the waitress was young and pretty. Whilst I went for the western, if unconventional, breakfast of burger and chips, Adam decided to be a little more exotic and go for chicken cooked in a Mexican style. Back at the hotel we tried, unsuccessfully, to get some more sleep and I called Bob, the Golden Gate Greeter, at 8 and arranged to meet him in the hotel lobby at 5.30 that evening. By 9 Adam had managed to start dozing so we didn't go to our planned first destination, Chinatown, until about 10. When we got there we spent a little time window shopping and sightseeing,

During our wanderings we came across a small park at St Mary's Square in the heart of Chinatown and took a few moments to sit on the park benches in the oasis of peace and tranquillity, only yards from the hustle and bustle of Chinatown. The park had a memorial plaque commemorating the Chinese from the city who were killed in the last war and an impressive tin statue of the first Chinese President, Sun Yat-Sen, by Beniamino Bufano.

After our relaxation in the park we headed into Chinatown to do some shopping. Adam bought a kimono for his Mum and I bought a motorcycle jacket in a leather goods store. The Chinese shop owner was a very pushy sales lady and was trying to sell a variety of clothes to Adam, none of which were to our taste at all. To avoid carrying our purchases around for the rest of the day, we took a taxi back to the hotel and dropped them off in our room.

We walked back to Chinatown and having decided that we wanted to try Dim Sum in San Francisco, headed for a Chinese restaurant, 'Gold Mountain', that was recommended in one of our guide books. The restaurant lacked character and looked rather shabby and run down. It was just a large room filled with cheap tables and chairs that were well past their 'sell by date'. The restaurant was very busy, but we managed to find a couple of chairs towards the rear of the room next to an elderly Chinese couple having their lunch.

Looking around I realised that we were the only non-Asians there and I thought that this would bode well for the food! Being the only non-Asians did have its disadvantages as it seemed that few of the staff or customers could speak English (or even American!), which made communication difficult. This became very apparent when Adam burned his arm on the metal tea pot and I wasn't able to summon any assistance. Fortunately the elderly lady next to us had noticed Adam's accident and called over to a waitress in Chinese and in a minute or so she re-appeared with some ice wrapped in a tea towel for Adam to cool his burn with. They were a nice couple and tried to engage us in conversation. We were able to conduct a basic conversation with the lady, explaining where we came from and that we would be touring, but we were unable to exchange more than a 'hello' in English with the gentleman, so the lady was translating, as best she was able, to enable us to talk with him. Adam didn't like his Dim Sum much and I had to admit to feeling a little nauseous after finishing the meal.

After lunch we caught a bus to Fisherman's Wharf to see if there was any music on at the Cannery. There was a saxophonist playing laid-back, easy listening music, a style that leaves both Adam and I cold, so after one drink and a couple of numbers, we caught a cable car back to the hotel. The brake-man, who also collects the fares, missed us out and so it turned out to be a free ride!

We met out Golden Gate Greeter, Bob Schneider, at 5:30pm, as arranged and initially walked west along Market Street to the Civic Centre. San Francisco's Civic Centre is a large plaza surrounded by a mixture of buildings housing civic, educational, cultural and art institutions. The dominant building, situated at one end of the oblong plaza and built of limestone, is City Hall which is surmounted by one of the tallest domes in America. Planning for the Civic Centre commenced following the great earthquake of 1906 however work on City Hall did not commence until 1915, spurred on by Congress making San Francisco the host city for the Panama Pacific Exhibition at that time. In the 1930s the War Memorial Opera House was built. Recently two new buildings have been added, the Library and the Court House. The opening of the new Library paved the way for the Asian Arts Museum to be relocated to the old Court House.

The Civic Centre was a magnificent sight. To see such a large open plaza amongst the rest of the crowded buildings in San Francisco gave me a feeling of peace and the surrounding architecture was a feast for the eyes. San Francisco has a diverse range of architecture, with each city district having its own, distinctive style. In the Tenderloin, where we were staying, and in the Financial District nearby, the architecture was mostly 'corporate box'. The change in the Civic Centre was marked and these were grand civic buildings in the old style, monumental in size, and designed to impress - I was duly impressed! Bob took us briefly into the new Library and then on a short tour through City Hall. If the outside of City Hall was impressive, the inside was even more so. The rooms were on a grand scale - large, bright and airy with high, impressive ceilings and marble floors.

After touring the ground floor of City Hall, we left by the rear entrance and Bob led us to the Western Addition district. This district is not part of the worn tourist trail and is more residential than any area that we had seen before. The area has Japan Town to the north and the houses on the south side are of a distinctive style known as 'Victorians' (because they were built whilst Victoria was on the throne in England) or 'Painted Ladies' (because of the bright colours that the residents have painted them). The residents living in the Western Addition are from a wide variety of the society of San Francisco - Straight, Gay, White, Black and Japanese. Whilst there are high levels of crime in some areas of the Western Addition, I found the atmosphere of the area that we walked through to be vibrant, friendly and refreshing and I enjoyed walking its tree lined streets and looking in the wide variety of niche commodity shops.

In the Hayes Valley (just South of the Western Addition), we stopped at one shop specialising in Japanese Sake and I bought a bottle, only to have it confiscated at the airport on the way home as I'd packed it in my hand luggage, completely forgetting about the anti-terrorist ban on liquids in hand baggage!

From the Western Addition we headed south to Mission by way of Fillmore Street and stopped for a drink in a small café. Mission has a strong Mexican / Latin feel to it, with many bars, cafés and 'taquerías' which serve Mexican fast food. I preferred the Western Addition to Mission as it had a less 'urban' feel to it and the streets seemed cleaner, but Mission had more going on - more to observe! After our drink we caught a bus from Market Street to Haight Ashbury, the old hippy hang-out. We got off the bus at the junction of Haight and Ashbury and walked up Haight to just before the intersection with Stanyan Street, looking in the hippy head and clothing shops along with the various cafés along the way.

Just before Stanyan Street we came to the place Bob had been leading us to - 'Amoeba Music' - an ENORMOUS record store. I guess that in floor area it is smaller than the Virgin Megastore, but it is crammed to the rafters with a wide variety of rare music in all formats: seventy-eights, vinyl, tapes and CDs, along with posters and memorabilia of bands past and present. Strongly featured are the bands that have played the Fillmore Auditorium and bands with a San Francisco connection. As it was late when we got there, we didn't stay too long but Adam still managed to find time to buy a CD before we caught a bus back to the hotel.

Adam seemed to attract the 'loony' on the bus. On the way to Haight Ashbury we had to stand, along with several other passengers, because the bus was full. As people got on and off we had to move to allow them access to the doors and it wasn't long before a transvestite began haranguing us about getting in the way and generally trying to draw attention to himself/herself. On the way back to the hotel a friendly drunk on the bus engaged Adam in conversation, about what I know not, but I don't think it was about the world's geopolitical situation! When we got back to the hotel we both had blisters from our four hour walk, but had enjoyed it immensely. We had put in our profile that we were interested in music and that we wanted to see some of the cultural highlights of San Francisco and "see San Francisco through the eyes of a local". Bob had exceeded our wildest expectations and had shown us a side of San Francisco that we would never have seen had we not had his expert local knowledge to guide us. I normally expect to get what I pay for. As this was a free service I hadn't expected anything much, but Bob's obvious enthusiasm, knowledge and pride in his city was infectious and I'd happily have paid for his services. He wouldn't even accept a tip when he dropped us off at the hotel! Thanks for sharing *your* San Francisco with us Bob!

We had booked a trip to Alcatraz at 11.30 on our last day, but Adam wanted to go back to Amoeba so we rose early, had a light breakfast of bagels and muffins in the hotel and took a taxi over to Haight Ashbury. We arrived just before 8.55 expecting the store to open at 9, which just goes to show that you shouldn't expect things like store opening hours to be the same the world over as the opening time was in fact 10.30! To fill in the time we went for a hobble (the blisters were still sore!) to Golden Gate Park. Because of our feet, we didn't go too far into the park but what we saw of it was very peaceful and well laid out with plenty of shade. The park is surprisingly large (1017 acres) and there are a wide variety of attractions and facilities within it, in addition to the beautiful surroundings. One website[2] lists 43 different activities and attractions that can be enjoyed in the park. There is even a buffalo paddock!

As we sat on a bench admiring the view we were surrounded by a flock of pigeons. As a walker approached all the pigeons, except one, drifted away from the path onto the grass. As we continued to watch the one remaining pigeon, we realised why he (or she) had stayed as two of the three toes on one foot were missing! Apart from this the pigeon seemed happy and healthy. We had also noticed the number of homeless people hanging around the park gate and in the park itself, but they all seemed very friendly and didn't cause us any bother; in fact some of them even wished us a cheerful 'good morning'.

Before Amoeba opened we took a walk down Haight and it was much quieter than it had been the previous evening, when the street was busy with all sorts of people passing to and fro and all of the shops, bars and clubs were open. There had definitely been a 'vibe' about the place then, but in the morning it was very quiet and sleepy with most of the shops being closed. Hippy hours I guess! Eventually 10.30 came around and we were waiting outside Amoeba with about a dozen or so other early rising music fans when the doors opened. As we needed to be on the other side of town in an hour, Adam didn't have much time to browse the vast collection of music available, but did find another CD to buy along with a couple of posters. He left the store with one CD and only one poster when he discovered, at the checkout, that the Nirvana poster he wanted was $50 (approx £27)!

At about 11.00 I telephoned the taxi to come and pick us up and he said that he'd be about 10 minutes. After 20 minutes I called him

---

2 http://www.sfgate.com/traveler/guide/sf/neighborhoods/ggpark.shtml

again to find that he was stuck in traffic. Fortunately an empty cab cruised by and stopped when I hailed it whilst still talking to the other driver! We were a little late arriving at Pier 33, but the ferry was delayed for some reason, so we ended up in a queue, waiting under a hot sun after our panicked rush to get there - a classic case of "hurry up and wait". The trip across the bay was only about ten minutes long but afforded great views of San Francisco, the Golden Gate Bridge, Bay Bridge and Alcatraz itself.

Seagull at Pier 39, San Francisco

On arrival at Alcatraz we were given a compulsory lecture about the island and its history by a Park Ranger. Alcatraz is now run by the U.S. National Park Service, who have done a superb job in bringing the history of this fascinating place to life by way of an 'audio tour'. Everyone is issued with a set of headphones connected to a box of electronic wizardry that hangs on a lanyard around the neck. There is a spoken commentary interspersed with sound effects and directions for moving around the jail. The walk up from the dock to the jail itself was quite steep and taxed our already overtaxed feet but the views across the bay made it all worthwhile. We entered the jail through the same door that the inmates would have crossed all those years ago and then entered the 'processing' area, which mainly consisted of open communal showers and a prison uniform store which was separated from the shower area by a chain link fence with hatches in it for the issue of uniforms.

The place was very sparse and utilitarian with bare concrete and brick walls, not at all welcoming. From the reception area we toured the cell area, seeing those that had held famous inmates such as The Birdman of Alcatraz (Robert Stroud), Al Capone, 'Machine Gun' Kelly and Henri Young. We learned of the escape attempts that had been made, some of which were imaginative and all were fraught with risk. Very few, if any, succeeded. Thirty six inmates tried escaping, in fourteen escape attempts. Twenty-three were caught, six were shot and killed during their escape, and two drowned, that leaves five who MAY have escaped, though most commentators believe that these men drowned in the Bay during their attempts.

The cells were very small, only 5' x 9' with an iron bar front prohibiting any privacy. Apart from an iron bedstead everything was screwed to the walls, everything being a small table / desk, a metal fold out seat, a couple of small shelves, a washbasin and a toilet. The cells were arranged in a 'block'; two rows of cells, two high, with the open, barred entrances facing each other. At one end of the block there is a gun gallery, some eight or so feet above the floor and protected by bars. This is where the armed guards patrolled, twenty four hours a day, watching over their charges.

Windows in the cell blocks were purposely sited in such a way as to prevent inmates from being able to view the mainland and civilisation. Their only view of San Francisco was during the rare periods in the exercise yard. Throughout Alcatraz the décor is spartan in the extreme, with bare painted walls and granite floors creating a cold, soulless, echoing interior. One of the most thought provoking parts of the tour is in a small corridor connecting adjacent blocks. Here you can see the marks on the floor and walls radiating out from a central point where a grenade exploded after it was dropped by guards through a gap in the ceiling onto the rioting prisoners.

The Alcatraz tour brought home to me how hard and unpleasant life would have been as an inmate of the world's most famous prison. From the draughts and cold, to the echoing institutional buildings, to the inhumane treatment meted out by the guards, to the constant infighting amongst inmates, it must have been a horrific life for those incarcerated, and I can understand why men rioted and attempted to escape. However we should remember that those locked away in Alcatraz were some of the most violent sociopaths that America had brought to justice who between them had been responsible for much suffering and many murders.

We were thwarted in our attempt to get a taxi on our return to shore when the disembarking passenger decided that he was in the wrong place and got back in. Five minutes later we were in another taxi headed back to the hotel via a roundabout route I believe, thus increasing the fare. I've not often felt that I've been duped in this way and, since the fare was not great anyway, I wasn't fleeced out of much money, but it's an annoying, if not unexpected aspect of being a tourist at the mercy of the locals seeking to make as much money out of tourism as possible. On the way we passed a homeless man shouting at passers-by as he was sitting in the street 'jacking up' in full view!

Back at the hotel we bathed and rested our tender feet, watching American TV and reading, before going to the Indian Restaurant across the street from the hotel for supper (we didn't want to walk any further!). To us Brits, who were used to the typical UK curry house, it was a strange experience. There were no waiters or waitresses, and so you had to go to the counter to order your food. They didn't have a license to sell alcohol (a liquor license in US parlance), and diners brought their own wine or beer but as we didn't know that, we were restricted to soft drinks. I had Saag Chicken (chicken and spinach) and Adam had Chicken Tikka Masala. My Saag Chicken was very good, and was a dish that I hadn't come across in the UK. Adam thought that his Chicken Tikka Masala was a little hotter than its UK counterpart, but enjoyed it nevertheless. Whilst we were waiting for our food to be served, a large procession of cyclists went down O'Farrell Street, escorted by police motorcyclists. At the time I wondered what it was all about, and after returning home found out that it was a part of 'Critical Mass'[3], a monthly

---

3 http://commutebybike.com/2007/04/05/clearing-the-air-on-san-francisco-critical-mass/

bike ride which takes place in cities across America, in protest against perceived anti-cyclist attitudes in cities. It appears that the one we witnessed was controversial due to an alleged incident between the cyclists and a van driver.

The following day we were going to collect the RV and head on to Yosemite. I was feeling fine - no more chest infections for me! We'd enjoyed our time in San Francisco but we were raring to go. I've now been there four times and have grown to love it more each time. I'm someone who doesn't generally like urban conurbations, preferring countryside, but I'd have to say that San Francisco is a place I'd make an exception for, and it is one of my favourite cities. The views are magnificent, the architecture interesting, the people are generally very friendly and there is a nice atmosphere. There is a thriving mix of cultures that make it an exciting city to visit and there are a great variety of cuisines from around the world to be sampled. It is a city where the sun (mostly) shines. On the other hand it is a city with a vast, tacky tourist industry catering to the most superficial. In the tourist areas you will be witnessing a 'show' and not actual life. The homeless beggars are a constant presence revealing a seamier side to San Francisco, but I never felt threatened by them. If you are prepared to seek out the 'real' San Francisco you will not be disappointed as it has something for everyone. I couldn't put it better than the Animals did in the first (spoken) verse of their song - 'San Franciscan Nights':

"This following program is dedicated to the city and people of San Francisco,
who may not know it but they are beautiful and so is their city.
This is a very personal song, so if the viewer cannot understand it,
particularly those of you who are European residents,
save up all your bread and fly Trans Love airways to San Francisco U.S.A.,
then maybe you'll understand the song,
it will be worth it, if not for the sake of this song but for the sake of your own peace of mind."

Chapter 15: Going Up The Country
(With Apologies to Canned Heat)

After rising, breakfasting and finishing up the packing, we were picked up at 9.15 by the affable Bulgarian who had collected us the previous year. There was another British family waiting for the shuttle in reception. They'd stayed at a hotel in Fisherman's Wharf from which El Monte didn't pick up, so were meeting the shuttle at Hotel Bijou. The father seemed a little concerned about driving an RV in America and we chatted for a while about the ins and outs of manoeuvring a large left hand drive vehicle on the 'wrong' side of the road. The journey followed the same route as the previous year and we were soon at El Monte's premises in Dublin. The manager, Gill, knew that we had rented from them before and 'fast tracked' us through the orientation and formalities - so we were soon on the road.

Last year our first stop had been the supermarket, but this year we drove less than a quarter of a mile before stopping at Arlen Ness's store to have a look at the bikes. Unfortunately the 'museum' upstairs was closed for a private party so we had to content ourselves with a look at the bikes for sale and the clothing and accessories. We both bought T-Shirts and then headed for the supermarket. I think that we were in and out in about 30 minutes and I was $260 (£135) poorer even though I had joined the loyalty scheme and got a discount on my purchases!

By now I'd installed the Sat Nav and had entered our destination - it was leading us to Yosemite. All was right with the world; the sun was shining; we had a stocked larder; the traffic was light on the I-580 and we had music on the stereo.

All this changed at 1.20 pm when we were about 16.5 miles from Dublin. My first indication was a big bang from the offside rear of the RV followed by a strong vibration coming from the rear. When I looked in my rear view mirror, I could see pieces of tyre tumbling along the Interstate. Fortunately there was a pull-in just up the road so I pulled off to assess the problem. It didn't take long to find it! The outside tyre (the rear axle had two wheels each side) had delaminated; this is where the tread parts company with the wires that make up the carcass of the tyre.

Part of the orientation lecture had dealt with punctures and the firm instruction had been – 'call for assistance!' Normally it would be the roadside assistance number that El Monte provided but as we were so near to the depot, I called them directly. After explaining the problem to them, I was asked to call back in ten minutes by which time they would have worked out the best way of helping me. Ten minutes later I was asked to drive slowly back to the depot on the three remaining wheels on the rear axle.

Back at the depot a mechanic changed the wheel for another one and I asked him to check the remaining tyre pressures since we'd had problems with one tyre. All were about 15 lb/Sq Inch too high and he let some air out of them to bring them to the right pressure. After a bit of haggling and a telephone call to the manager at his home, El Monte agreed to refund a full day's rental fee because of the problems.

At 3.15pm we set off once again for Yosemite. At Tracy, about 30 miles from Dublin, we stopped for a late lunch at a Jack in the Box and stopped again a little further down the road for the butter and stock cubes that we'd forgotten to get in the supermarket. By 6.15pm we were still about 35 miles from Yosemite and as I'd had enough for the day, we stopped at Yosemite Lakes Resort.

The Camp-ground was only one part of a large resort that had both cabins and yurts for rent. Yurts are quite a common form of accommodation around Yosemite and are basically a substantial round tent with a latticed wooden frame. The site had a shop, gas station and pavilion as well as tennis courts and the Tuolumne River running through it, which can be used for fishing and kayaking in the summer months. A few days before our arrival, the bridge over the Tuolumne River had broken under the weight of a heavy lorry and this was causing some problems for the site owners as they had to relocate people who were staying on the far side of the river.

We levelled the RV with the ramps provided and connected the services. When I turned the tap on for the mains water, I noticed that there was a deluge of water coming from underneath the RV. A quick look confirmed my worst fears as the pieces of de-laminated tread coming off the tyre had damaged the underside of the RV and punctured the fresh water tank! With the tank punctured neither mains water nor on-board water worked, so there was no water in the taps.

Damage to the on-board fresh water tank caused by de-lamination of a tyre

I tried calling roadside assistance, but my mobile didn't have a signal (we were, after all, out in the boonies!). The lady receptionist was very sympathetic, even offering me a scotch, and insisted that I use her personal land-line to phone for assistance. Unfortunately when I got through, I got a recorded message telling me that they were closed for the night and this was at 7.15pm! I could just as easily have broken down on the side of an interstate! We were therefore stuck until the following day when I could hopefully get someone to come and help us. Fortunately, as we were planning on camping later, I had brought a collapsible water container with us so we were able to 'camp' in our expensive RV. To wash up we had to boil water in saucepans, but it all added to the adventure!

It was obvious that nothing could be done to repair the RV without major surgery, so we would have to swap RVs just like we had to last year. Knowing this I did not want to unpack our suitcases which meant that we had to keep them inside the RV, rather than in the locker accessed from outside, underneath the fixed bed. This made the space cramped and difficult to find the things that we wanted as inevitably, the thing we needed was at the bottom of a suitcase or rucksack.

I'd put some potatoes on to cook and then we'd changed our minds and decided to eat later. I thought that I'd turned them off, but later found that I hadn't, and that we had a watery potato soup lurking in the supposedly 'switched-off' saucepan. Instead of the expected mash we had new potatoes and steak in a red wine sauce for supper - very nice! Adam was in bed by 8.20pm, an unheard of time for him! It got quite cold in the night and I had to put the heating on to keep us warm.

We had a simple breakfast of toast and coffee the next day (almost no washing up!) although making the coffee proved challenging as I'd forgotten to buy any coffee filters. I improvised with a mesh bag that had previously contained onions, which I folded over to give overlapping layers that decreased the size of the holes, making a rough and ready filter. The coffee was a bit 'gritty' but at least it was coffee!

After settling the bill with the camp-site, we started back for Dublin with Adam watching the mobile phone for any indication of a signal. We finally found a signal at Big Oak Flat, about 35 miles from Yosemite Lakes. I rang roadside assistance, who didn't seem to comprehend quite what the problem was but said they would call me back in thirty minutes. After forty minutes I hadn't had the promised call so called them back to be told there was nothing that they could do for me as it was Sunday, and could I call them again the following day at 8.00am? Not wanting to waste yet another day, I asked if I could exchange the RV for another back at the Dublin depot of El Monte and was told that the nearest depot was closed and I would have to wait until the following day. Before calling Roadside Assistance and waiting for the callback (that never came) I had called the Dublin depot of El Monte and spoken to Al. He had advised me to call Roadside Assistance, but to call him back if I needed any further help and after drawing a blank with Roadside Assistance (sic) I did just that. He was most helpful saying that he was quite happy to exchange the RV, but could I call him back in ten minutes so that he could check that there was a replacement RV available. Ten minutes and one phone call later, we were on our way back to Dublin.

We stopped for lunch at a Del Taco (fast food outlet specialising in Mexican food) and arrived back in Dublin for 1.00pm. I was most careful this time to ensure that I had transferred ALL of our belongings to the new RV before setting off!

We left at about 2.00pm heading back towards Yosemite. The new RV seemed fine but I was worried about the coach battery, (the one that powers the 12 volt electrics in back of the RV as opposed the battery that supplied power for the engine and road lights) as it seemed low on charge. I needn't have worried as it didn't give any trouble for the remainder of the trip. We stopped at the same shopping mall in Oakdale as on the outward journey, but instead of visiting the Del Taco we went to the supermarket and bought some supplies for the RV (including coffee filters!) and a cup of coffee to keep me awake for the rest of the trip.

Both the outward and return journeys were uneventful. The roads weren't interstates and so average speeds were quite low, but the scenery was stunning in places. Unfortunately, the circumstances surrounding the journey took the edge off the spectacular scenery for me. The only thing of interest was that the sat nav took us on a slightly different route from the one we had taken on the outward journey. On the return journey we went through more of the mountains and I had to concentrate to ensure that I didn't miss a curve and end up at the bottom of a cliff! The mountain route was a little shorter, but MUCH steeper. I'm not sure why the sat nav should take two different routes, but it did add some variety to an otherwise boring and wasted day.

We arrived at Yosemite Lakes at around 5pm and were allocated the same pitch as the previous night. After settling in, without a river flowing from the underside of the RV, I cooked a spaghetti bolognese using buffalo meat. Buffalo meat has a stronger flavour than beef and so gave the bolognese an interesting flavour. Whilst I was cooking, Adam had collected firewood and after supper we lit a fire in the fire pit. A family from Essex in a large RV hired from El Monte, had pitched next to us and were having problems with the electrics. They seemed a little lost so we gave them a hand to get the electrics working before returning to our fire and turning in for the night. We were both excited at the prospect of achieving our aim of wild camping in Yosemite the next day. Unfortunately we were to be disappointed yet again!

Chapter 16: Yosemite Sam
(With Apologies to Mel Blanc)

The spaghetti bolognese that I had cooked the previous night was both unusual (because of the buffalo meat) and tasty; fortunately there was some left over which Adam and I had for breakfast. We then settled up with the camp-site, put some petrol in the tank at the camp store and headed for Yosemite Park. The petrol was $3.69 per gallon, which was comparatively expensive compared with the petrol we had bought so far, so we didn't fill the tank and only (only!) bought $35 worth. Americans were complaining about the price of 'gas' wherever we went and $3.69 was the most expensive we had encountered so far (later on we were to pay over $4 per gallon). $3.69 equates to about £1.90 per gallon and we were paying about £0.90 per litre at the time in the UK which equates to a little over £4.00, or $8.50 per gallon. As an imperial gallon is a little more than a US gallon, (a US gallon is approximately 0.83 imperial gallon) the cost of a US gallon in the UK would therefore be about £3.30 ($7) about twice as much as it was in the US, and they were complaining!

After about 15 miles we arrived at the Park entrance and paid $20 for entry, which enabled us to stay for seven days. A pass covering all US National Parks for one year was available at $80 but as we were only planning to go to one other National Park (Death Valley), which would cost us another $20, it wasn't cost effective.

Five miles from the gate we stopped to take a picture of a particularly impressive view but I couldn't find my camera! Adam and I undertook a panic search of the RV, but the camera wasn't anywhere to be found. With a heavy heart I turned around to go back to Yosemite Lakes in the hope that it would be somewhere on our vacated pitch, or that some kind, honest soul had handed it in to reception. I wasn't overly hopeful but had to try as it had all of the pictures that I had taken up to that point stored on its memory card. As we returned, the family who had been having trouble with their electrics passed us heading the other way. I was overjoyed to find the camera sitting on top of the mains hook up post on our old pitch. Our pictures were safe (and I was saved having to fill in insurance forms in triplicate)!

So with camera on board we turned around, retraced our steps and an hour later I was able to take a picture of the view. After another 17 miles we arrived in Yosemite Village intending to visit the information centre, not only to get information but also wilderness permits and a bear canister. I also needed to get a camping stove.

As we arrived in the Village we were able to see the views that we remembered so vividly from last year in all of their glory, as the sun was now shining. We stopped to take some pictures and, as we were returning to the RV, our electrically challenged friends stopped to tell us that we had left our camera on the pitch and that they had placed it on the hook-up post for us to find! We thanked them profusely and explained that we had already retrieved the camera. They may have been electrically challenged but they were kind and honest! What goes around, comes around; we helped them with their electrics and they did the decent thing with our camera.

El Capitan from the valley floor

The Ranger in the visitor centre was very helpful and we discussed with him the best places to go wild camping. Our first choice was Hetchy Hetchy, but after he had checked with their Ranger we were advised that it wouldn't be a good idea to take the RV up the Hetchy Hetchy road as it was being repaired, making it difficult to get large vehicles through.

We therefore changed our plans and decided to go to Wawona and hike up in the hills behind, following the course of the Chilnualna River. The Ranger told us that we could get a bear canister at the Wawona Store and a Wilderness Pass at the Wawona Information Station at Hill's Studio in the grounds of the Wawona Hotel. Thus informed, we had a burger for lunch at the Village Grill before catching a free shuttle bus to Curry Village to buy a stove at the Mountain Shop. We found a suitable stove for $22 (£12), which took a threaded gas canister ($5 / £2.75) with a valve on it so that we could remove the canister and take the stove home after our trip (hoping that we could get a suitable canister in the UK, which we later found that we could).

With full stomachs and furnished with information and a stove, we set out for Wawona, a 30 mile drive along a winding road complete with sheer drops and another set of breathtaking views. We were planning to stay at the Wawona Camp-ground but found that it was full on our arrival, so we looked at a map and found another Camp-ground about 5 miles down the road. However, when we eventually found it, having missed our turning, it was closed.

Our next plan was to find a camp-site using the sat nav and it found one about 25 miles away, which we headed for. On the way I saw a Yosemite Visitor Centre and we stopped to see if they had any camp-site information, which they did and pointed us at a camp-site two miles further on down the road, the High Sierra RV Park on the bank of the Fresno River. High Sierra RV Park is located close to the centre of Oakhurst and our pitch backed on to the river. We hadn't been settled long when a large 'fifth wheel' RV pitched up next door and had some trouble pitching due to the restricted turning space. The couple alleviated the problem by using walkie-talkies, with the lady directing the driver into the optimum position 'over the air'.

Whilst I cooked supper, Adam collected firewood so that we could light the fire-pit later in the evening. There was plenty around on the riverbank and he had little trouble in amassing sufficient for a decent fire. Whilst he was collecting, another rental unit pitched next door and the Dutch couple in it asked if we were planning to have a fire (the fire-pit was located between the two pitches). When we said yes they asked if they could join us and offered to contribute some of their shop bought firewood. The couple had a five month old baby who was very good natured, quiet and well behaved. I doubt I would have had the confidence to take a five month old baby on a long international flight and then tour a strange country in an RV!

We spent a pleasant and enjoyable evening around the fire talking about our respective countries and our travels. The lady was a psychologist and had obviously travelled extensively. Her husband worked for a pharmaceutical company and they had been touring California and Nevada for two weeks and had one week left of their three-week vacation. We discovered a common interest in beer and shared a variety of bottled local brews, comparing them with the beers we were used to from our respective homes. We parted company at about 10.30pm when the fire started to die down and had a shower before retiring for a peaceful night's rest (or so I thought!).

Shortly after midnight I was woken by a shrill, repetitive, screaming sound. It took me a few moments to realise that it was the LPG (gas) alarm so I got up and pressed the mute button, but the alarm sounded again just as I got back into bed. I repeated this a couple of times before fanning the area near the alarm with a towel in an attempt to disperse any gas that may have been causing the alarm to trigger. I couldn't smell any gas, so wasn't too worried. Fanning the air didn't help and the alarm soon started to go off again, so I opened the door and fanned some more. It soon became cold and so I shut the door and waited for about five minutes to see if all was well now - blissful silence. I went back to bed but as soon as I did the alarm went off again!

Enough was enough - it was time to read the manual! This didn't help much as I'd already done everything it suggested apart from turning off the gas, which I then did. Five minutes later the alarm went off again. This was getting beyond a joke. I was very conscious of the young baby next door and didn't want to wake her, no more than I wanted to be awoken myself. The manual's final suggestion was to ring roadside assistance, but previous experience had demonstrated that this would be pointless at one am!

I finally resorted to more drastic measures so using the potato peeler as a screwdriver, removed and disconnected the alarm unit. I felt quite safe in doing so as the gas was turned off at the tank. The downside of this was that we couldn't put the heating on and it was now cold both on the outside and the inside as I'd kept the door open for so long trying to silence the alarm. We were both rather cold the next morning, but at least we had uninterrupted sleep for the rest of the night! When we got up I reconnected the alarm and waited for fifteen minutes before turning on the gas again. The alarm remained silent. Some unkind people who know me have suggested that the alarm may have been set off by liberated intestinal gases, but I refute this accusation strenuously!

It had been our intention to return to the Wawona Camp-ground to see if we could find a vacated pitch where we could park the RV whilst we camped in the mountains behind. We had discussed this with the Dutch couple around the fire the previous evening and they had expressed the view that this sounded like a good idea and that they would be interested in camping in Wawona.

As we were washing up after breakfast, the Dutch couple pulled off of their pitch and I became concerned that they would get any vacant pitch on the first come - first served Wawona Camp-ground. However when we left about ten minutes later they were parked outside reception and hadn't actually left the site. It was all academic however as there were no pitches available for either of us (the Dutch couple showed up at the Camp-ground about ten minutes after us).

I needed petrol so pulled up at the gas station in Wawona, filled up and asked Dan the attendant if he knew where we could leave the RV overnight whilst we camped. He didn't know of anywhere but suggested that we ask a Ranger and helpfully called one at the South Gate who said that we could leave the RV at the Chilnualna Trail-head provided that we put all our food and toiletries in the free bear boxes provided in the Trail-head car park. We did a quick 'recce', found the car park and bear boxes and then went to the Wawona Store to hire a bear canister.

Disaster! The store only carried bear canisters in the 'high' season, and the nearest place we could get one was in Yosemite Village! We'd been told at the Visitor Centre in the Village that we could get a canister in Wawona but now we were being told in Wawona that we needed to go back to the Village! It took us three hours to get back to Yosemite Village, hire a canister, stock up on money and supplies and return to Wawona, where we arrived at about 1pm. We obtained our Wilderness Permit, had a quick lunch of tinned chilli, deposited the rest of our food and our toiletries in the bear boxes and set out for the hills with our rucksacks on our backs.

After eighteen months of planning and a multitude of setbacks and trials, we were finally achieving our goal of hiking, with a view to camping in Yosemite!

To get to the trail-head we had to go through the residential part of Wawona, where the locals lived. Most of the houses were of wooden construction and were set amongst the trees, with plenty of space between each property. There was a strong community atmosphere, with typical community buildings, such as a fire station, library, school and general store in evidence. A significant proportion of the houses had a Ranger's truck or pick-ups parked on the drive showing the significance of the National Park to this small community. As we drove through I thought what a wonderful place it would be to live, or to grow up in.

A sunny Yosemite from Tunnel View

The early part of the hike soon brought us to a spectacular waterfall but the trail was VERY steep and taxing me greatly - it was even slowing Adam down unless he was being kind to his old, unfit Dad! The weather was very hot and this didn't help as my legs were refusing to work after every steep climb and I had to stop for a rest before they would respond to my orders again! Adam commented in his diary: *"Dad had problems with the trail as it is steep and rocky in places, and VERY hot."*

I had tried to mark the position of the Trail-head on my hand held GPS, but couldn't pick up any satellites - so I gave up. I continued to try and get a signal whilst on the trail but to no avail, and was forced to navigate by dead reckoning and comparison of the features on the ground with those marked on the map. In the UK, walkers and hikers use Ordnance Survey maps, which are of excellent quality, with a wealth of useful detail. However US maps do not seem to be so detailed, even those considered to be the 'Rolls Royce' of US maps; the US Geological Survey topological maps. This lack of detail was hampering my efforts at map reading but the trail was well marked and it would have been unlikely that we would have lost our way on the return journey, even without the benefit of a detailed map. It just felt alien to be walking in a wilderness without the benefit and comfort of knowing precisely where I was and being able to mark it accurately on a detailed map so that I could quickly plan a route back to civilisation; especially in the event of some unforeseen emergency or to let the emergency services know exactly where I was.

After the initial steep climb the trail became much easier, always rising, but in a much gentler fashion, not like the almost vertical slopes of the lower trail. As we walked we encountered a series of views across the mountains and valleys that literally, after the strenuous walking, took our breath away.

We continued walking for a while and, if my navigation and the map were to be believed, we would soon face another steep climb. My legs were voting VERY strongly NOT to do any more steep climbs, and my lungs and heart were seconding the vote, so we started to look for a suitable camp-site. After another mile or so we found a suitable location next to a fallen tree about fifty yards from the river. It seemed to me that it was the first six square feet of level ground that we had seen since starting out.

View from the Chilnualna Trail with a Manzanita bush in the foreground

We had to clear some dry fallen branches from the site, but these made good firewood later. I also moved some earth from one side of the site to the other in order to level it off a little more, as sleeping on even gently sloping ground usually means that the two of you end up in a huddle against the tent wall on the lowest side of the tent when you wake up!

Preparations complete we then put up the tent and placed the bear canister, full of food, next to a fallen tree about thirty yards away. By placing the canister away from the tent you can ensure that you maintain a safe distance from any inquisitive bear, and you are less likely to get between the bear and the food that it knows is there. If you kept the canister in the tent, the bear would join you in your temporary home, most likely entering via a wall rather than the door, to get at it. Not recommended for a restful night's sleep!

Neither of us felt like eating at this point, so having collected more firewood and explored our local environment, we went for a walk which was much easier without heavy packs on our backs! Adam found evidence of recent bear activity down by the river (pug marks and faeces) and was quite excited about it although I wasn't so sure, wondering if the bear would return! When we returned to camp Adam sorted the firewood into tinder, kindling, small branches and large logs to make fire lighting easier later on, then we played cards for a while.

Whilst Adam was sorting the firewood, I managed to get the GPS working. I'd forgotten to change the time zone; when I did, I was gratified to find that my dead reckoning position was the same as the GPS position. With the GPS working, I used it to check when sunset would occur and it was predicted to be at 19:21 - and so it proved to be.

We lit the fire at about 19:40 and it started well. We had built a fire-pit on a flat rock that stood just proud of the ground in front of the tent by using rocks placed in a circle to contain the fire. Most people in this situation would go for a big roaring fire and, whilst a big fire is satisfying, it is wasteful of firewood and is more likely to get out of control. So we kept a small steady fire, sufficient to keep us warm by adding small pieces of wood when necessary. Towards the end of the evening Adam wanted to add a larger log to get a bigger fire, and as it was getting later and we wouldn't be keeping the fire going for much longer - we did.

Chilnualna camp

The log was too long to fit entirely into the fire-pit, so it extended outside of the circle and only burned at one end but it gave plenty of heat and light. At about 10.00 pm we decided to let the fire die down and go to bed. By 10.30 the fire had died down enough for us to tidy the embers, including the unburned end of the large log, into the middle of the fire-pit and get into our sleeping bags. About thirty minutes later we noticed that the fire seemed very bright through the walls of the tent, so Adam got up to investigate, but all was well as it was only the log end flaring up, and it was well contained within the fire-pit and was quite safe.

Despite night time temperatures being reported to be down to zero we weren't cold and I had a good night's sleep and didn't need to get up for a pee. I normally need to get up at least once in the night, and this can be a bit of a problem when you're in a small tent in the wilds. I'm quite a big bloke and getting out of a small tent whilst finding my boots and putting them on in the dark is difficult and inevitably it also wakes Adam up, so I was glad that it wasn't necessary this time.

I had sterilised some river water with iodine tablets on the previous day so that we had some water to make a breakfast brew with. Previously I'd always used chlorine tablets, but needed to use iodine in Yosemite because of the giardia. I found that the taste of the water with iodine was better than the chlorine taste (I used neutralising tablets with both types of sterilisation), so will be using iodine all the time from now on!

For breakfast, we had a couple of tins of what was claimed to be 'roast beef hash' and it burned a little on the bottom of the pan. We both found it rather tasteless, apart from the slightly burned taste, and Adam left his. One of the rules about wild camping in Yosemite is that you must carry out everything that you take in with you (pack it in, pack it out) so, to avoid having to carry the leftover food back to the RV, I ate his as well. Despite the fact that I burned the hash, the new stove worked very well and I preferred it to the stoves we used at home.

After breakfast we struck camp and set about ensuring that the site looked as though no one had camped there. We distributed the fire pit rocks around the surrounding area and did the same with the ashes and left-over fire wood. There were some soot marks on the rock that we had built the fire on, but they would disappear after a couple of rains. I'm quite particular about leaving a camp in the condition that it was found and where there is grass on the ground, I remove turfs with a trowel, saving them so that we can replace them when the fire is out, thus preserving the area. Many people also forget that a fire can smoulder underground in loamy soil areas, so we always spike the ground well with a stick and pour plenty of water into the resulting holes to ensure that the fire is well and truly out. In Yosemite this wasn't necessary as we built the fire on rock, which was quite cold in the morning.

The hike back to the trail-head was considerably easier than the hike out, as this time gravity was our friend and being earlier in the day, the air was cooler. Back at the RV we retrieved our food from the bear box, had a well-earned cold drink, changed our socks and then returned the bear canister. Fortunately there is a canister drop off behind Hill's Studio, so we were saved having to make the round trip to the valley floor to return it. Adam was very keen to see the giant sequoias, so we then headed off in the direction of Mariposa Grove, which is famous for its sequoias.

On our second attempt, eighteen months after the first, we had managed to fulfil our dream and had wild camped in Yosemite. We'd wanted to spend another night camping in Yosemite, but the time taken locating a camp-site and bear canister prevented this.

The walk up the steep hills in the heat had taxed me to my limit, and had even slowed Adam down, but it was worth it! It was a wondrous and magnificent experience to be in such a pristine wilderness amongst nature, hearing the birds and creatures that inhabited Yosemite and seeing the stupendous views that could only be seen by hiking up into the wilds and that would never be seen by vehicle bound sightseers. The views from the valley floor are beautiful, but are always seen from the perspective of a 'spectator'. Hiking in the hills puts you 'in' the landscape and allows you to see, and experience, the majesty that is Yosemite from a much more personal and intimate perspective. It was an experience that will live with me, and Adam, for the rest of our lives and I am grateful to have had the opportunity to have been there.

"Take nothing but memories and photographs, leave nothing but footprints."

Chapter 17: Up Around the Bend
(With Apologies to Creedence Clearwater Revival)

At the park gate, on the way to Mariposa Grove, we were stopped and asked about the length of the RV as there is a length limit on vehicles there, but it appeared that we were just on the maximum length and were allowed in. We realised why there is a length limit when we got there and saw the car park! Only a few spaces were long enough to accommodate our RV and they were all taken! Fortunately the car park attendant helpfully directed us to the coach parking area after advising us not to spend too much in the souvenir shop on expensive guides as the cheap $3.50 guide (Harvey, H. Thomas, The Sequoias of Yosemite National Park) was as good as any of the more expensive guides.

Being a little short of time (and a little footsore!) we didn't walk too far, but within a mile of the car park we saw seven of the more famous sequoias. The first is called the 'Fallen Monarch' and, as the name suggests, the tree has fallen. It is estimated that it fell over three hundred years ago and is 15 feet in diameter, 10 feet above the base. It would have been much bigger in diameter when alive as it is now only heartwood as the outer layers of sapwood and bark have decayed.

The next trees that we saw were all in a tight group of three that grow very close together and are known as the "Three Graces". This is uncommon with most other tree species as normally they compete with each other for light and root space; however Sequoias often grow close together in small groups of up to ten trees so that their root systems interlink and thus support each other. All of the three trees are over 200 feet tall, with the tallest reaching nearly 260 feet.

After admiring the Three Graces, we walked on to a tree called the "Grizzly Giant", the largest and oldest tree in the grove; it is estimated to be between 2,500 years and 3,000 years old and is the fifth largest tree on earth (by volume). It is a little over 200 feet tall and measures 92 feet, around 8 feet above the ground just above the buttresses.

The last of the famous trees that we visited was the "California Tunnel Tree". The first tunnel tree was the Wawona Tree, which is the one that people are most familiar with from the old pictures of a car being driven through it. The tunnel was made in 1895 and the tree fell in 1969, but a tunnel had been cut through another tree, the California Tunnel Tree, in 1909 and this one still stands.

After our short visit to Mariposa Grove, we set off for Death Valley. We didn't expect to make it all the way to Death Valley that day but did want to get some miles under our belts before nightfall. The Sat Nav wanted to take us over the Tioga Pass but we knew that was closed from bitter experience the previous year! To stop the Sat Nav annoying us by incessantly repeating "Turn around when possible" every mile or so, I turned it off and then headed south for Fresno. At Fresno I turned the Sat Nav back on and it calculated a route that took us through Bakersfield.

As we got further south the surrounding countryside began to change in nature, going from lush green to dry, dusty brown with sparse vegetation. Towns became smaller and further apart. From wooded upland we had come down to desert. The temperature was also rising until it became quite hot and after going up one rather steep hill, I had to stop to let the engine cool down as it was starting to overheat.

The RV documentation recommended that you turn off the air conditioning when going up long steep hills to take some load off the engine, which I had done, but the temperature still rose into the red, so I pulled off into a lay-by and we admired the view for 10 minutes or so whilst the engine cooled. The lack of air conditioning and standing around outside the RV caused us to overheat too! The heat felt different from the hot weather in the UK, where it is quite humid when the temperature rises. In California it is a dry heat so you don't sweat so much and, for me, this makes it much more tolerable.

Shortly after joining the I-14, we saw a sign for the Sierra Trails RV Park and decided that after 278 miles, the first few of which were on foot in the hills of Yosemite, we would spend the night there.

As our fresh food had gone off in the bear box in Wawona, we needed to get some supplies in before settling down for the night so drove down into California City which is a mile or two off the I-14. It was a straggly, dusty sort of town with buildings well spread out and a slightly unkempt air to it. After driving up and down the high street a couple of times and branching off into a couple of side streets we had been unable to find a major supermarket. The only shop we could find was a small, family run supermarket with a limited choice of goods. However we were able to get some meat, bread and butter to keep us going until we could find a better-stocked supermarket.

It took us a while to find the RV Park, despite having directions, but we eventually found it. It was a strange sort of park, seemingly a mixture of residential RVs and tourers like ours. After connecting the city water, I found that it was leaking at the union with the RV. The guy in the RV next to us noticed and said that he had a spare sealing washer in his RV and went to find it. Whilst he was away I found some sand stuck to our washer and managed to stop the leak.

When he came back with the washer we got to talking for a while. He and his wife lived in Idaho and were touring California. Like us they had just driven down from Yosemite and were going to visit family about 80 miles from the site. They were a friendly couple and were most interested to hear of our adventures. It was nice of them to have offered us the sealing washer when they saw we had a problem and I hope that they had a pleasant visit with their family.

Having seen, and been unimpressed by California City, we foolishly decided that we would be better off eating in the next nearest town, Mojave. After having a much needed shower we drove into Mojave and found 'Mike's Diner', which had a large parking area where we could park the RV, so we unwisely decided to have dinner there! Adam decided to have liver and onions with mashed potato, which came with a starter of potato soup, and I went for the rib eye steak with a salad starter. Adam had one spoonful of his potato soup and left the rest declaring it "disgusting".

When the main courses arrived they brought me ribs instead of steak and I had to wait whilst they cooked me a steak. Unfortunately while they were cooking the steak, they didn't do anything to keep my baked potato warm and it was cold when they returned my meal. After the meal Adam ordered a banoffee pie but a couple of minutes later the waitress came back to say that they were out of banoffee pie but they did have fudge sundae, which Adam agreed to. Two minutes later, unrequested, the bill arrived! I asked about the dessert and the waitresses admitted forgetting it and let us have it free of charge because of all of the cock ups. For the first time in America I didn't leave a tip!

When we got back to Sierra Trails I noticed that it had filled considerably, and most of the new arrivals were towing trailers with dirt bikes on, there were also some dirt bikes being ridden around the site. There were also more road bikes (all Harleys) than I would have expected by mere chance. I never found out for sure but guessed that there must have been some sort of race scheduled for the following day.

At about 1am the LPG alarm went off again, waking us up. Enough was enough, so I removed it permanently until the day we returned the RV!

After our disturbed night's sleep, we had a (comparative) lie-in until nearly 8am and decided to stop for breakfast on the road and, looking at the map, decided that our best bet would be Johannesburg, about 35 miles up the I-14. On the way we went through a curious town called Randburgh. It looked like a ghost town, or maybe a film set. There were many abandoned and derelict buildings, but there were also some that looked lived in and an open shop (I subsequently found out that it has a population of 80, but we didn't see anyone). We stopped and explored for a short while and took a few pictures before bemusedly resuming our journey.

We were unable to find anywhere to eat in Johannesburg, which turned out to be not much more than a village. We therefore kept going, intending to eat in the next town – Ridgecrest - 22 miles down the road according to the map, where we did eventually find somewhere to eat. It was a diner run by a family of Mexicans and they provided us with a very welcome US fried breakfast.

From Ridgecrest we took Highway 1-78 towards Death Valley. This was a road that we had driven down last year, but this time when we reached the end we would be turning right, towards Death Valley, instead of left, away from Death Valley, as we did last year. When I saw the long chain link fence of the China Lake Weapons Research Centre the memories started to flood back. I remembered travelling through the two dustbowls of Argus and Trona and listening to Nirvana as we travelled through the desert looking at the colourful geology exposed on the valley sides on the entrance to Panamint Valley. As I drove along reminiscing, we were both startled by a Harrier and F16 flying, in formation, at less than 100 feet altitude directly overhead. I don't know about Adam, but I jumped as they suddenly materialised over us with a roar!

Shortly before reaching Trona, we stopped at an information sign at the side of the road giving details of the 'Trona Pinnacles'. These are 10,000 – 100,000 year old calcium carbonate pillars rising from the dried up bed of the Searles Dry Lake, about five miles down a dirt road off the metalled road we were on. The tallest pinnacles are around 140 feet high and the area has been used as a backdrop to many science fiction movies (Star Trek - The Final Frontier and Planet of the Apes amongst others) due to its 'other worldly' landscape.

It sounded interesting so we decided to make the ten mile detour, but after only a few hundred yards we discovered that the dirt road was like a washboard and looked like the hard, rippled sand that you sometimes see on the beach after the tide has gone out. This set up an immense vibration in the camper, severely shaking both the contents and ourselves at whatever speed I drove at. Conversation was impossible - it was uncomfortable and at a speed of less than five mph it would have taken us an hour or so each way, so we gave up, turned around, and rejoined the main road heading for Trona. I had been looking forward to seeing this strange geology, but we couldn't afford two hours out of our day, plus sightseeing time, nor could we have put up with the vibration and noise in the RV. Given past experiences with the RV(s), I'm pretty sure that the vibration would also have broken something!

We stopped briefly in Trona to clean the windscreen and get some soft drinks before setting out for Furnace Creek, by way of Stovepipe Wells. This brief stop confirmed the impression that I had formed last year that I wouldn't want to live here. It was hot, dry and dusty. The views across the dried-up lake bed were all spoiled by the mineral extraction plants and machinery. I could taste the mineral dust in the air! The cashier in the service station was chatting with another local and looked at us as though we were something that she had stepped on and found stuck to the bottom of her shoe. Not a friendly welcome!

As we headed east on the Death Valley Scenic Highway, the opposite way from that which we had taken last year, the road started to rise as we crossed the Panamint Mountains. As the road rose, so did the engine temperature! When the temperature reached 250°F (121°C) I turned off the air conditioning, which seemed to help; however, after we had stopped for a couple of minutes to take a photograph, the temperature went off the scale briefly when I restarted the engine, so I turned it off again and we waited for ten to fifteen minutes to allow it to cool a little before setting off again.

At Stovepipe Wells we did a little shopping, buying some souvenirs and then having a lunch of the ubiquitous cheeseburgers at the wonderfully air-conditioned restaurant. We chatted to the waitress and, when we commented on the heat, she told us that this was the 'cool' season and she was longing for the warmer months ahead! She was also looking forward to the weekend when she was going to visit family in Yosemite where she thought the cooler air would make a pleasant change!

As we left Stovepipe Wells, we stopped at the National Park ticket machine to buy our permit ($20 for 7 days). There was a thermometer next to the machine and it was reading 100°F (38°C) in the shade (the same as the hottest recorded temperature in the UK: Sunday, 10th August 2003 in Gravesend, Kent[4]). A few miles out of Stovepipe Wells we passed through the Devil's Cornfield, an area covered solely with strange plants, the 'arrow weed' (*Pluchea Sericea*).

These look like overgrown grass tussocks, are about three and a half feet tall and can grow to a height of ten feet. Native Americans used the long straight branches to make arrows, hence the name. The shape of the bushes made me think of a pepper pot, so the area looked like the storage area in a pepper pot factory!

As we travelled to Furnace Creek, we saw a group of motorcyclists coming the other way. There were about eight or nine touring Harleys, all with pillion passengers. As the last of the bunch approached us the woman on the pillion lifted up her T-shirt, revealing her bra-less boobs to us! I wish we were both travelling slower as it was all over in a '*flash*'! Shortly before Furnace Creek we

---

4 http://news.bbc.co.uk/1/hi/uk/3138865.stm

stopped off at the Harmony Borax Works. Borax was a major product for Death Valley in the late 19th Century and used in a variety of ways: In the household it was used in laundry and cosmetics. Industrially it was used in pottery, biochemistry, metallurgy, as a fire retardant, insecticide, fungicide and also as a flux.

The Borax Works graphically showed us what it would have been like working out in the desert with minimal resources. Just strolling around the open air museum left us both tired and exhausted from the energy sapping heat. What it would have been like to have worked hard all day in the heat and then have to return to a tent for the night instead of an air conditioned, fully equipped RV, I can't begin to imagine.

Harmony Borax Works – Twenty Mule Team

A couple of miles from the Harmony Borax Works lies the village of Furnace Creek where the Death Valley Visitor Centre is located and we spent an hour or so there. The exhibits gave a good insight into the history, people and geology of the area and opened a small window onto the fascinating place that is Death Valley. The most striking feature of Death Valley is its topography and geology. It's not a true valley, more a plain, running south west to north east between two mountain ranges, the Panamint Mountains to the west and the Black Mountains to the east. The geology of the area is a geologist's dream, having undergone many major upheavals in the past; two glacial periods, four periods of sedimentation (meaning that the valley was, at those times, underwater), tectonic upheaval involving subduction (where one tectonic plate rises over another), subsidence and four volcanic periods.

The highest point is Mount Whitney at 14,500 feet (4,400m) and the lowest is at Badwater, 282 feet (86m) below sea level which is the second lowest point in the western hemisphere. This height difference between two points, located only 85 miles apart, gives the largest elevation gradient in the US. Death Valley National Park was established in 1933 and covers 2,250 square miles (7,700 km^2) . In 1994 another 1,650 square miles (5,650 km^2) was added, giving rise to a 3,900 square mile (13,500 km^2) park covering Death Valley and the neighbouring Panamint Valley.

The geological features of a low plain bordered on two sides by mountain ranges, and the direction of the prevailing winds, causes a rain shadow effect, where warm moist air coming off the sea cools as it is forced to rise over the Panamint mountain range. As the air cools it condenses, forming clouds, which then release the water as rain (or snow) on the upward slope of the range, leaving dry air to blow over the top of the range. This means that little or no rain falls in the lee of the range - Death Valley. This rainfall shadow means that Death Valley is one of the driest and hottest places on earth, with summer temperatures regularly reaching 120°F (49°C) or higher, and an annual rainfall of approximately 1.7" (43mm) at Badwater.

Given the paucity of rainfall, and the high ambient temperatures, it is surprising how many plant and animal species call Death Valley their home. There are 1,040 plant species, 51 species of mammal, 307 bird species, 36 reptile species, 3 amphibian species and, surprisingly, 2 fish species! Twenty three of the plant species are found nowhere else on earth.

The earliest known human habitation was by Native Americans, specifically the Nevares Spring People who lived a hunter-gatherer lifestyle here, 9000 thousand years ago. The Nevares Spring People were replaced by the Mesquite Flat People around 5000 years ago, followed by the Saratoga Spring People 2000 years ago. 1000 years ago the area became inhabited by the Timbisha (AKA Shoshone). The Timbisha moved between the valley floor and the mountain slopes according to the seasons, making maximum use of the available resources. The Timbisha are known for their basket making skills, many of which are incredibly detailed and beautiful as well as watertight[5]!

The appalling treatment of the Timbisha by the US Government over the years is, unfortunately, similar to the treatment received by other tribes across America. Following the arrival of settlers the Western Shoshone signed the 'Treaty of Ruby Valley' in 1863 allowing the US *access* to their land; however, it should be noted that this treaty did not *transfer* ownership of the land, only grant access. In 1933, following the establishment of the Death Valley Monument, the area was run by the National Park Service who began moving indigenous people onto a 40-acre plot of land on the valley floor where nine adobe houses, a trading post and a laundry were later built. This small plot of land was then home to the tribe for nearly sixty five years.

The tribe received federal recognition in 1983 which meant that they were able to receive funding for the improvement of their land and buildings. Subsequently, in 1994, the California Desert Protection Act was passed which provided for the provision of 'suitable' land for the tribe, within their traditional lands. In 1996, following an internal evaluation, the National Park Service declared that there was no 'suitable' land. The tribe took action and notified the press of their predicament. The ensuing media interest resulted in the National Park Service revising their position, now stating that they were willing to work further with the tribe to "work out a long term lease". After lobbying President Clinton directly, 7,500 acres of land were finally transferred into trust for the benefit of the tribe, in the centennial year.

---

5   http://www.timbisha.org/basket_gallery_01/index.htm

The California Gold Rush started in 1849, giving rise to the term 'forty-niners' for the prospectors who rushed to California in an attempt to literally find their fortune. Two groups of these forty-niners who had lost their way, ended up in Death Valley whilst attempting to find a short cut. Because of the surrounding mountains, they were unable to get out of the valley for several weeks and had the greatest difficulty surviving in the harsh climate and barren landscape, resorting to burning the wood of their wagons as firewood and killing some of their oxen for meat. When they finally found a way out of the valley, via the Wingate Pass, one of the group said "Goodbye Death Valley" thus bestowing a European name on the valley (the Timbisha name is Tümpisa, meaning "rock paint").

In 1881 borax was found in Death Valley and the mineral extraction industry began. The Harmony Borax Works (q.v.) were built in 1883 and the borax it produced was used in industry to make soap. It was carried 165 miles to the nearest railway at Mojave by so-called "twenty mule trains" which actually comprised eighteen mules and two horses.

These 'trains' hauled a load of 10 tons of borax in the wagons; the large tank is the water tank to supply the mules, horses and men of the train during their thirty day trip. The whole train weighed in at over 36 tons and was over 100 feet from front to back. In subsequent years other minerals, such as gold, silver, lead and copper were discovered and mined for a while, but the harsh climate and remoteness of the valley made these ventures untenable in the long term.

Our permit allowed us to claim a free map at the Visitor Centre, which we did before setting off for our overnight camp-site at Tecopa Springs RV Park, which we selected from one of the camp ground magazines. I'd estimated that the park was about 30 miles from the Visitor Centre, but when I programmed it into the Sat Nav, I found that it was nearer to 60; however the straight, traffic-free road meant that we made good time and arrived shortly before 4pm.

The receptionist was knowledgeable about the locality and told us about the area and the springs. Our site fees, good value at $17 (£10) per night, included free use of the springs and this sounded like heaven to me as all the driving had left me with a series of aches and pains throughout my body! The reception also had a small store selling essential food items and locally made souvenirs, where Adam bought a pottery vase as a present for his Mum.

After settling in, I left Adam revising for his forthcoming exams whilst I went for a soak in the springs. There were two bath houses, his and hers, because of the no swimming costume rule. Whilst changing I got talking to a couple of local guys. They were talking politics and were both vehemently anti-Bush, one claiming that Bush "wasn't his President" and that he "didn't know anyone who had voted for him". The other claimed that the election had been "rigged" and that "Bush orchestrated 9–11". He said that Bush's foreign policy "sucked" and that "Bush should be given a fair trial before being hanged". He continued that he "wasn't proud to be American since Bush had come to power" and that he was "ashamed for his daughter to be brought up under a Bush administration". Quite forthright opinions!

The soak in the springs was very relaxing and eased the aches and pains wonderfully. I felt much better when I returned to the RV and Adam and I took a walk to look at the salt pan behind the camp ground. We had a supper of steak and pasta before retiring for an early night. Whilst the soak in the hot springs had settled my aches for then, the aches were soon to reappear in one area of my anatomy with a vengeance!

Chapter 18: Viva Las Vegas
(With Apologies to Elvis)

Our plan for the day was to drive to Las Vegas where we had reserved a rental Harley which we were due to collect on the following day. As it was a comparatively short trip of around 100 miles, we felt that we could have an easy day. We therefore made a slow start to the day, having a lie in and, for me, a cooked breakfast of bacon, sausages, baked beans and a fried egg in the RV. Adam didn't have breakfast, but did have a longer lie in!

On our way to Tecopa we had passed through the village of Shoshone and, after topping up with fuel ($100 (£60) for half a tank!), we visited the small museum opposite. Despite its size it had a wide variety of exhibits ranging from the skeleton of the Shoshone Mammoth, believed to be a male over 500,000 years old, to an exhibit illustrating the history of women in Death Valley. Geology, human history, natural history and the history of Tecopa plus Shoshone and its museum were also covered. Entrance was free, but donations were gratefully received and I was happy to donate to such a worthy local museum - well done guys!

Now educated in the history of Shoshone and the surrounding area, we set off for Las Vegas, a journey of about 90 miles. There was a completely different 'feel' and 'atmosphere' when we had crossed the state line into Nevada. The landscape was subtly different; flatter and somehow dustier. The road itself was better maintained than the roads that we had been driving on in California and there were more advertising hoardings lining the roads, mostly for casinos and brothels and it wasn't too long before we passed a brothel. It was larger than I would have expected, and was very 'in your face' with large signs proclaiming its function - not at all furtive as an Englishman might have expected!

I was surprised at the amount of building work going on. There seemed to be developments every few miles along the road; houses, shopping malls, more casinos, and probably more brothels!

We made a short stop in Pahrump to buy some socks for Adam, as he hadn't brought sufficient with him, and some provisions for the RV. Initially we stopped at a JC Penny outlet store, but they didn't have any socks; however, the lady assistant was very friendly and helpfully directed us to a nearby Super Store. We had quite a chat with her before continuing with our shopping.

Our route took us over the Spring Mountains which, whilst picturesque, did not compare with the High Sierras and Panamint Range in California. As we approached Las Vegas, we stopped at a 'Sports Bar' for a late lunch. The bar was full of giant-sized flat screen TVs showing about 10 different sports channels and was decorated with sports memorabilia. It was quite distracting to have so many different sports showing on adjacent sets. It was like being in a TV store, with all the display TVs showing different channels!

I chose Alaskan snow crab and Adam had chilli. Neither of us could finish our meals - they were so large! I have a particular fondness for Alaskan snow crab, believing it to be the finest of crabs but unfortunately it's difficult to find in our area of the UK, so I take every opportunity to eat it whilst in America. I highly recommend it!

Despite the Sat Nav, I managed to take a wrong turning on a freeway on the outskirts of Las Vegas and we were slightly delayed finding the RV site as the Sat Nav had recalculated a longer route. The site I had picked from the RV sites magazine looked very nice as we drove in to it but unfortunately it was full. Fortunately the receptionist directed us to another site about half a mile up the road and we managed to get a pitch there.

They only had a couple of pitches left, and those could only accommodate 'small' RVs and as luck would have it our RV was considered minute by American standards. The pitch we arrived on would have accommodated an RV twice our size! The site, Arizona Charlie's, was part of a casino / hotel / RV Park complex and it was all concrete and asphalt, with small plant borders dotted around and the pitches were close together, but at least we had somewhere to stay for the night.

Shortly after arriving we met Mark who was in the RV opposite. He worked at a nearby nuclear fuel repository (not a comforting thought!) and basically lived on the site working for a six week stretch before returning 'home' to his wife in Colorado for a week and then returning to Arizona Charlie's for another six weeks.

We got chatting because of the Harley parked outside his RV. He told us that he had another five motorcycles back in Colorado, but this Harley was his favourite and he proceeded to show us all the 'custom' parts that he had ordered out of a catalogue and fitted to his bike. We told him of our plan to hire a Harley and asked him for advice on the best roads to ride. His response was to offer us a beer, which we gratefully accepted, and suggest that we all go for a ride on the following day, and he would show us the best roads from the saddle, which seemed like an excellent idea. Unfortunately it never happened. I saw Mark the following morning whilst checking the LPG level and he said that he'd remembered that he'd booked his pick-up truck in at the air-con workshop and wouldn't be able to come for a ride after all!

We went to the casino restaurant for supper and it was typically American, I think that I had chicken wings or similar. To get to the restaurant we had to go through the slot machine hall (we would wouldn't we?) and it looked very depressing to me. Rows and rows of gleaming machinery with a few people sitting on stools in front of some of them, repeatedly feeding coins into the slots. Not my idea of a good time, but if it keeps them happy and off the streets ...

The following morning we were too excited to eat breakfast and were at Las Vegas Harley Davidson just as they opened. Apparently (according to Mark) Las Vegas Harley Davidson is the biggest Harley dealership in the US. I don't know if he's right, but it certainly was very big. The rental processing operation was very slick and we were passed from one employee to another as various stages of the process were completed. The last process was being shown the bike and being asked to take a riding test. I wondered what this would involve - a ride around town being followed by a tester? An off road test track perhaps?

When it came to it all I had to do was ride about twenty yards down the car park, "make a wide turn", and ride back. Some test! As I headed back up the car park after making my "wide turn", the tester gave me a big grin and put two thumbs up - apparently I had passed the test and we were free to go. I had parked the RV in the car park (by prior arrangement) and we stopped off to load the panniers with toiletries and fresh underwear before "heading out on the highway".

With Mark's advice we had decided to ride over to the Hoover Dam before riding down to the Mojave National Preserve but first we toured around Las Vegas looking at the sights along the 'strip'. It all looked very gaudy and tacky to me. As we were riding around Las Vegas, both Adam and I became aware that the Harley's suspension was set too soft and constantly bottomed out when we went over bumps and potholes. It also had limited ground clearance when going around right hand bends: Because of the compressed suspension, the exhausts scraped on the road even at modest angles of lean, and this, coupled with a minimally padded seat would cause us a lot of discomfort on the coming ride!

On the 30-mile ride to the dam, we stopped off at a 'Jack in the Box' for a late breakfast of $^1/_3$ lb 'Angus Burger' (with bacon and cheese). With stomachs re-fuelled, we continued to the dam but found long traffic queues leading up to it due to road works near the dam. We stopped to see the view across the top of the dam and decided to turn around and head back. You can get through traffic better on a motorcycle than in a car, but it's not a lot of fun. The dam was narrower and taller than I expected and the lake it creates, Lake Mead, was a deep blue and had many skiers and jet skis on it.

On the run up to the dam I'd seen an advert by the Dam Helicopter Company for flights over the dam for $29 (£17.50) and thought "Why not?", and asked Adam whether he'd like to go. Unsurprisingly he said 'yes' and we stopped at the booking trailer. I discovered that the $29 flights didn't go over the dam; they were just a 'come on' and were for a two minute flight over the lake. The five minute dam flights were $59 (£35.75), but you don't get the chance to fly in a helicopter over the Hoover dam very often, so I bought a couple of tickets.

We had a bit of a wait because the pilot needed to make adjustments to the helicopter and refuel (or, more likely, have lunch!). Whilst waiting, Adam and I got talking with a family from Carshalton who were staying in Las Vegas. They seemed very taken with the glitz and glamour of Las Vegas, but didn't seem interested in the local history, people or countryside. I thought to myself that we had travelled half way around the world to meet a family who didn't share our interests or views on life but lived less than 50 miles from us!

After a short wait it was our turn. We were driven the 20 yards to the helicopter pad as were told it was a rule that we had to go by car but I suspect it was a way of keeping the general public away from the nasty whirring things on helicopters that can seriously ruin your day if you walk in to them. In our case it didn't matter as, unlike the previous flights, the engine was off. This gave us more of a chance to chat to the pilot without the noise of the running engine as he went through his engine start procedure and pre-flight check-list. We chatted about the bike and how it compared to my Honda back home (the Harley was more agricultural, didn't perform as well, didn't handle as well, vibrated more and was more uncomfortable). Adam spotted that the pilot was wearing a 'Nam Veterans' baseball cap and asked him about it. It turned out that he had learned to fly helicopters in the army and had seen action in Vietnam. I'm sure that, had we more time, he could have told us a tale or two, but by this time we were set for take-off.

The Hoover Dam from low altitude

I've flown in a lot of different types of aircraft, passenger jets, military transports, single and twin- engined light aircraft and even have a glider pilot's licence, but I'd never flown in a helicopter before. It vibrated less than I'd expected (and less than the Harley!) and the manoeuvrability in the hover was a revelation. To me it felt very odd to be flying backwards and sideways at a very slow airspeed.

It had always been drummed in to me that flying below the stall speed of the aircraft (i.e. slowly) was a sure-fire way of turning a flying machine into a feature of the landscape. As an observation platform it was superb, and the pilot obviously knew how to use the helicopter's characteristics to best effect in order to display the lake and dam at their best. The views were superb and were well worth the $118. I could seriously get hooked on this helicopter flying!

Adam was in the co-pilot's seat, which left me with a more restricted view from the rear seats; however the lack of other passengers meant that I could look out from either side to obtain the best view. We hit a little turbulence as we passed over the sun-heated rocks (which create thermals) on the shoreline of the lake on the way back but the landing was beautifully smooth. The only bad thing about the flight was its short duration!

Following our return to earth, we pointed the front wheel of the bike southwards on the US-95 in the direction of the Mojave National Preserve. This took us down the eastern side of the Preserve and resulted in great views to our right as we rode along. It also resulted in strong cross winds coming off the flat terrain of the Preserve, buffeting the bike as we rode along. At times I had to lean the bike over a fair way into the wind just to maintain a straight course and the gusts literally took my breath away, as my nostrils acted like venturi with the wind passing at 90° across them.

We were riding directly into the sun, which made visibility difficult and it made our eyes tired. At one point we hit a bump so severe it caused the suspension to 'bottom out'. The jolt was so severe that I almost lost my grip on the handlebars and it caused Adam to shoot upwards, out of his seat. He was worried that he would fall off the back! That bump was the final straw for our numb bums and I started to look for a suitable place to stop so that we could regain circulation in our rear ends. Before long a turning appeared and we pulled off the main road onto what we thought was just a minor byway and found a place to stop. It turned out that our 'minor byway' was in fact the original 'Route 66' which was now a part of the National Trails Highway and celebrated in the song 'Route 66' by the songwriter Bobby Troup and sung by Nat King Cole, Chuck Berry, the Rolling Stones and others.

As we rested our sore posteriors, I started to walk out into the deserted road to take a picture when a car came into view. As I stepped back to the roadside, the driver must have thought I was trying to stop him as he pulled up and asked us if we were OK. I assured him that we were, explained our reason for stopping and he went on his way, chuckling to himself as I took my picture. We soon realised that the road ran alongside a rail track as a long goods train passed. When I say 'long' I mean LONG! In Southern England the engine would have been in one local station whilst the rear of the train was in another. I timed how long it took to pass and it was nearly five minutes, albeit moving quite slowly. The whole train must have been several miles long!

Resting our bums on Route 66!

Route 66 showed its heritage and age and proved to be very pot holed and bumpy, which didn't help our sore rear ends and we were glad to see a gas station cum general store cum burger bar after about 14 miles. It was very remote but we hadn't seen a store or a gas station for miles until we came across this one. We filled up the bike and then headed for the burger bar to fill up ourselves.

Whilst waiting for the inevitable cheeseburger, I wandered around the general store and bought myself some sun screen to put on my face, which was now sore with incipient sun burn. Although we had changed direction to the west, so had the sun with the passage of time, and I was still riding full on into it! The store was quite strange and very expensive. They had a sign by the till that said "*If you don't like the prices, you don't have to shop here. Our overheads are very high, with high rent and high transportation costs, so we have to pass these costs on. Please do NOT complain about the prices to the cashier.*"

There were also many back copies of "The Watchtower" piled on every table in the diner section. However strange and pricey, I was glad to see it as we needed gas, sunscreen, liquid and food and it provided all four as well as giving us somewhere to rest our weary backsides. As we were finishing our burgers two coach-loads of tourists arrived and I was glad that we'd both visited the loo earlier in our visit, as everyone from the buses immediately headed in that direction. The queue for the ladies must have had at least fifty to sixty people in it, and whilst the gents queue moved faster, it started out a similar length!

Leaving the coach tourists to their queuing, we set out for Kelso at the centre of the Preserve. The difference between a National Park and a Preserve is that you can hunt wild game in a Preserve but not in a National Park. Kelso used to be a train depot and this is just about the only thing in Kelso. This is where 'helper engines' were attached to trains to enable them to get up the Cima Grade more quickly. The track up Cima Grade rises two thousand feet in eighteen miles, which is a steep climb in railroad terms. Apparently bandits used to throw goods off the trains as they slowly made their way up the grade and this booty was then retrieved by their associates.

The old depot house, which has startling Spanish architecture, has been restored and converted into a museum and visitor centre.

Unfortunately they closed at 5pm and we didn't arrive until 4.30pm so only had time for a whistle-stop 'run' around before closing time. It's a shame as it looked to be an interesting place. When it was a working depot, the building not only housed the offices, but also housed the workers. The museum had workers' bedrooms preserved as they would have been in the depot's heyday, which was an interesting glimpse into the lives of the original inhabitants.

Feeling sore, sunburned and shattered, our bums endured the remaining 35 miles to Baker with the aid of a couple of rest stops. Baker, when we got there, was a small 'strip' town spread out along a mile or so of I-15. Its claim to fame is that it has the world's biggest thermometer, which commemorates the world's highest ever thermometer reading, taken in Death Valley, of 134°F and is accordingly 134 feet tall with a maximum reading of 134°F.

As we turned into town, we saw a Motel on the left hand side and headed straight for it despite its generally run down appearance. The check-in was in the adjacent store and the welcome less than effusive. They simply asked me to fill in a form and then carried on serving shop customers. When the form was complete, they relieved me of $74 and gave me a key. A 'no frills' approach to customer service!

The room was quite large and badly in need of redecoration. The door lock was 'temperamental' and often refused to release the key after the door had been unlocked but the beds were comfortable and both the air con and the TV workèd. I thought $74 (£45) was a bit steep for what we had, but there wasn't a lot of choice, so I guess that market forces are alive and well in Baker and a shortage of supply had led to a hike in prices. We were just glad not to still have a constant vibration and pounding on our nether regions. I'm probably labouring the sore bum thing, but it really is my most vivid and enduring memory of the day!

We had a look at the Motel restaurant and the Greek restaurant across the road, "The Mad Greek", which purportedly sold the "best gyros in the US", but neither appealed. I don't know what a gyro is, but the décor, food on display and queues prevented me from finding out. About half a mile up the road we found 'Coco's Restaurant and Bakery' and both elected for the jambalaya. It was quite pleasant, but not the taste I remembered from previous jambalayas and it gave Adam heartburn!

Chapter 19: Pacific Coast Highway
(With Apologies to the Mamas and Papas)

We breakfasted on an 'all you can eat buffet' for $8.95 at the Motel restaurant and then took the most direct route to Las Vegas (the I-15) because of our (still) sore bums. Even on the comparatively smooth Interstate, we had to stop a couple of times to ease the aches. By the time we got to 'Vegas our bums were so sore that we took the bike straight back, despite there being a half day left on the hire.

Back in the RV we retraced our wheel tracks down the I-15 towards Los Angeles, intending to follow the Pacific Coast Highway north back to Dublin to drop off the RV a few days later. The I-15 was rather boring and Adam slept for a couple of hours before we stopped for food near Calico just outside Barstow. The couple from Essex that we had met whilst waiting for the helicopter flight had recommended a visit to Calico, but it sounded as though the main attraction was a stage managed cowboy show for the tourists and this didn't appeal to us, so we didn't bother to visit Calico itself and just ate at the 'Jenny Rose Restaurant' on the service area.

The Jenny Rose Restaurant is a Mexican restaurant that appeared to have recently opened. It was very clean and the food was excellent, as was the service. Adam and I both decided to try steak fajitas, but weren't too sure what we'd get. Whilst we waited for the main course we were given tortilla chips and salsa. The salsa was wonderful, very fresh and nicely spiced - not too strong but with a 'bite'. The waiter noticed that we'd finished the salsa and brought us another bowl. When the fajitas arrived they were a revelation. I'm a convert! This was without a doubt the best meal we'd tasted in America! Following our return I bought a book on Mexican cooking and we're gradually learning to cook the dishes, though the ingredients can sometimes be hard to come by. The internet helps greatly in getting some of the more esoteric ingredients and we're now all becoming rather fond of Mexican food.

After the meal we continued towards Los Angeles but the weather took a turn for the worse. Up until now we'd had good weather with bright sunshine. Now the wind made its presence felt. It had been windy on the bike, but not as windy as we were experiencing at this point. The RV was being repeatedly blown off course and the wind had raised a dust cloud which was like a thick fog with severely limited visibility. Scary stuff! We were approaching the San Bernardino Mountain range and the wind abated as we climbed higher into the range; however, by the time we had reached the top, fog had closed in around us and visibility was again limited. We had seen clouds above us as we were driving on the lower slopes; now we were in those clouds. The fog thinned as we descended, but never truly dissipated.

I had been undecided as to whether we should stop before driving through Los Angeles, or whether to press on to the coast but, as we got nearer to Los Angeles, the traffic got worse and we found ourselves sitting in traffic jams. I then decided to make an early stop and programmed the Sat Nav to take us to an RV park. When the Sat Nav proudly announced that we had reached our destination, there was no RV park, only a quarry, so I programmed it to take us to the next RV park and it took us to a quiet suburban street with kids playing ball and riding their bikes! Giving up on the Sat Nav I looked in the parks magazine and found one, Terrace Village, about 10 miles from where we were.

When we got there the office was closed but they had left details of 3 vacant pitches with envelopes to put the payment in. It was a bit expensive, at $40 (£24) per night, but I'd had enough of running around and it was after 6pm on Easter Sunday so I stumped up the cash, put it in the envelope, posted it through the letterbox and we settled in.

The site was well maintained, but very suburban, with units packed quite closely together. The pitch we were on was very small by American standards, and we only just managed to fit our RV into it. That didn't really matter as we were only 'over-nighting' before pressing on in the morning. Our supper was a family favourite: roasted pork chops with mustard and sage accompanied by mushy peas and boiled potatoes. After driving the bike for nearly 100 miles and the RV for another 250, I was quite tired so fortunately Adam did the washing up and then we retired early!

The previous year we had stopped at Neptune's Net for lunch when we were on the bike and as it was only about 80 miles from us, we decided to stop for breakfast there. We left the site at about 9.00 am and the Sat Nav predicted arrival at Neptune's Net just after 10:30. However, we soon hit a major traffic jam on the interstate just north of LA and after about 30 minutes in the jam we reached the cause - a motorcycle accident. The bike was totalled, with the front wheel and forks plastered up against the front of the engine. As we were approaching we saw an ambulance pulling away with its lights flashing and the sirens wailing. I hope that the rider was OK.

At Malibu I saw a petrol station on the other side of the road and, being low on gas, made a U-turn to go back and top up. As I did so there was a loud crash from the back of the RV and the pots and pans drawer came out and deposited its contents on the floor. Adam went back to sort it out and was promptly hit by the falling bunk ladder! Quite an eventful 100 yards! It turned out that the drawer runner was broken and so we had to rearrange the pots and pans and jammed the broken drawer closed, which caused confusion whenever I was cooking during the remainder of the trip! 38 Gallons (US) and $132 (£80) later we were back on our way to breakfast.

We arrived at Neptune's Net at around 11am and it was just as we remembered it. Adam, predictably, went for the cheeseburger but, as Neptune's Net is famous for its seafood, I decided to go for the fish, clams and chips. The clams were particularly good. They were cooked in a way I'd never had clams before - deep fried in breadcrumbs - and though I'm not a big fan of deep fried food in breadcrumbs (I hate the British dish, deep fried scampi and chips in a basket), I really enjoyed the clams as they tasted of the sea and were so fresh.

After our meal we hit the road again and headed north. From LA to Neptune's Net, and then for a few more miles, the road follows the coast and has spectacular views as the curves of the road open up vistas of craggy headlands with bays nestled between. The road then turns inland and the scenery becomes less impressive, consisting mainly of flat farmland divided up into large fields of unidentifiable crops. The weather had started misty but it was brilliant sunshine when we got to Neptune's Net. As we headed north from Neptune's Net, the wind began to pick up again and was blowing the RV about so before long we were again driving in a dust storm which limited visibility. The dust got everywhere and I could taste it in my mouth and feel the grittiness between my teeth.

I was beginning to worry that we were slipping a little behind schedule and I didn't want to be late getting the RV back to Dublin and, following on from that, miss our flight. I was probably being over cautious, as is my nature when it comes to travelling. I'm cautious this way because I've been stuck in too many traffic jams, got hopelessly lost too often and had too many breakdowns (especially in California!) to leave my schedules too tight. Up until now, with the exception of Las Vegas for the bike rental, it hadn't mattered when we arrived, or even if we arrived at our destination, but missing the flight home would have been a financial and logistical nightmare!

Because of my concerns I elected to continue on the main interstate, I-101, rather than take the more scenic coast road when the roads divided just north of San Luis Obispo. Having decided on the faster route, I checked the sites directory and found a suitable site at Paso Robles - the 'Wine Country RV Resort'. I'd like to say that the name had nothing to do with my decision, but I'd be lying if I did!

When we got to the resort we found it to be well laid out and maintained. The receptionist was friendly and chatty and I made a slight error of judgement when I decided to ask her about local restaurants. This would be our penultimate night in the US and, like last year, we were planning to have our farewell meal then as the last night would be spent at Del Valle, far away from a 'posh' restaurant.

The receptionist was trying to be helpful, but couldn't seem to get the idea of a 'posh' meal. However often we said 'not burgers', she didn't seem to grasp the idea and kept referring us to restaurants specialising in burgers and other fast foods. A particular favourite recommendation was a local 'Irish' bar that specialised in (you guessed it!) burgers! I've been to Ireland and, whilst I have very fond memories of the excellent produce and restaurants there, I don't recall seeing, or eating, burgers there, nor have I heard that Ireland has a reputation for excellent burgers! The reason for the recommendation was the short skirts of the waitresses, which she thought that Adam would like. I'm sure he would have (so would I!) but we were after a quality meal, not visual stimulation. Eventually the receptionist gave up on making her own recommendations and gave us a copy of a local tourist guide newspaper which listed local restaurants. The reception area had a wide variety of goods for sale, as demonstrated by my purchases: A bottle of (pricey) local red wine (a Zinfandel) and some toilet chemicals!

After we had pitched Adam spent some time in the shower, and then spent more time trying to get the tangles out of his hair caused by yesterday's bike ride. He not only lost time, but also a significant quantity of hair! We then spent some time pouring over the newspaper guide considering the possibilities it revealed. Finally we decided to visit the Paso Robles Inn for our 'end of trip' meal.

The Paso Robles Inn was an inn with attached steakhouse furnished and decorated in an old colonial style which I found very relaxing and comfortable. We both had excellent meals - Adam choosing 'Kansas Steak' which came on the bone with rosemary crushed potatoes, and I had the halibut in wine in a dill sauce. Halibut was a favourite fish dish of mine when I first started living with my wife. After I told her of my fondness for halibut, we had it every other day for a couple of months. Whilst I appreciate the sentiment, and love her for it, I became less fond of halibut for a while and haven't had it much since (mainly because of the rising price), but this one just 'touched the spot' and I loved it. We both had Tiramisu for pud' and even got a discount because of the delay in serving it (which we didn't mind anyway!).

On our return to the RV park, Adam went straight to bed (unusual for him) and I tried a glass of the Zinfandel which was very good and worth the high price! Tomorrow we would be on the home run.

Chapter 20: Run For Home
(With apologies to Lindisfarne)

Our last full day in America! We started with a solid, home (or at least RV) cooked breakfast of bacon, Irish garlic (!) sausages and range type baked beans (which have chilli added), to which I added a little basil and butter. Baked beans in America are a bewilderment for anyone from the UK. There are so many different types! In the UK we basically have one type of baked bean: the Heinz type in tomato sauce. There is a small selection of additives (e.g. cocktail sausages) but that's about it; all the other manufacturers produce much the same product. In the US it's very different as there's a whole aisle in the supermarket dedicated to baked beans! None of which, or at least none I've tried, are anything like the UK offering. First it's the sauce they come in. There are loads of different sauces for baked beans in the US, but none seem to be the same as the sauce I'm used to from UK baked bean tins. Then it's the beans; they're just BIGGER than baked beans in the UK. That's not to say that they are all bad, some are rather nice, like the ones we had for breakfast, but they're just not baked beans as I know and love them.

We left Paso Robles at about 9am with the intention of putting some miles under our wheels as quickly as possible. We had about 200 miles to travel before arriving at Del Valle and we wanted a bit of time spare when we arrived to pack for the flight the next day and to clean the RV as there wouldn't be time the following morning.

We were about half way to Del Valle when Adam spotted a sign for the town of Solidad, which is the location for the book 'Of Mice and Men' by John Steinbeck, which Adam was studying for his English exams. We couldn't pass up such serendipity and turned off to go and have a look at the town. We drove around for a while looking at the sights and stopped a couple of times to take pictures. The final time we stopped for a picture I found that I couldn't get the RV into gear when we came to leave! I thought it was because we were parked on a slope and the gearbox had jammed in park because I hadn't applied the parking brake. I'd had this happen to me before in automatic cars in the UK and the usual remedy is to get someone to 'rock' the car whilst you attempt to get the gearbox out of park. Not too bad in a car, but a little more difficult with an RV weighing over 5 tonnes! Adam and I pushed and pulled for all we were worth and managed to get the RV rocking quite well, but I still couldn't get it out of park! Eventually I admitted defeat and we had to call the breakdown assistance number.

It didn't take too long for a tow truck to pull up and I explained the problem to the mechanic. He got in the RV, started it and put it into gear without any trouble whatsoever! I was astounded until he explained that Dodge gearboxes have a fail-safe linked to the foot brake, and you couldn't get it out of park until you put your foot on the brake. I must have done it automatically up until this time without realising! With a very red face I thanked the mechanic profusely and apologised for getting him out on a fool's errand.

The remainder of the trip to Del Valle was uneventful, the only thing of note being a glitch in the Sat Nav where it showed our position to be a couple of hundred yards to the left of the road. Had it been accurate we would have been driving at 60 mph across fields of crops! It kept this up for several miles before suddenly correcting itself and showed us that we were now driving on the road!

We stopped at Livermore for some petrol and, for the first time on the trip, I checked the petrol consumption: 194 miles / 28.472 US Gallons = 6.81 mpg! Americans were moaning about the price of gas at $4 (£2.50) per US gallon; however, this would have cost around $8 (£5) in the UK. I'm sure glad that we weren't driving the RV in the UK!

On arrival at Del Valle we found that there were no serviced pitches (with mains water and sewage facilities) available. I was quite surprised at this as last year we were just about the only people on the site.

Del Valle was as beautiful and tranquil as I remembered it, perhaps more so since the sun was shining. We had a quick lunch to use up the tinned stew although we had planned to have this in Yosemite, but hadn't eaten it and had been carrying it around California since then. With the addition of some herbs and garlic, it was almost palatable!

The packing and cleaning went better than I'd feared, to the point that I thought I'd forgotten something! I always try to leave a little space in my suitcases when packing for a trip as I know that I'll be buying something, be it souvenirs, or goods that are cheaper abroad, or just plain unobtainable in the UK. On this trip Adam and I had bought a leather motorcycle jacket, a set of bamboo steamers, a silk kimono for Simone, several T shirts and several smaller presents. In addition to these we had half a dozen leftover tins of food and several packets of herbs that we would be taking back with us. I wasn't at all sure that I could fit it all in, but somehow I did (the bamboo steamers were packed full of socks when I put them in the suitcase)!

Any useful leftover goodies such as the bottled stuff (including beer!), which I didn't pack, I put in a bag and took to the people on the pitch next door (actually about 50 yards away). They were an elderly couple and they seemed a little wary of us at first, but soon became friendly when we explained why we had come to see them and were grateful for the bits and pieces that we could no longer use. I binned the opened packets of food and fresh vegetables.

Chores done, Adam and I went for a last walk down by the lake, stopping on the way for a chat with the elderly couple on the next pitch who were keen to hear our impressions of America. They were stopping at Del Valle for a couple of days on their way from Palo Alto on a tour of California.

Del Valle lake

It seemed to me that the lake was a little low on water compared to our previous visit, but it still shone and glittered in the sunshine. Despite the serviced pitches being fully booked, along with the bright sunshine and the astounding beauty of the spot, we only saw one other couple walking down by the lake. It seemed a shame that so many people were missing out on the view and peace of the lake, but this was to our benefit, allowing us both to reminisce about our time in America and savour our last few hours there in peace and solitude. On the way back to the RV, we saw lots of eagles circling on the thermals above us, but I had used all of the memory in my camera, and so wasn't able to take any pictures of them.

On our return to the RV, we took a shower in the shower block, which was rather cold, and then had a supper of buffalo steak, pasta and sweetcorn accompanied by the remainder of the Zinfandel. Afterwards we made a fire in the fire-pit and indulged in a little fire gazing, adding the large local fir cones every ten minutes or so which caused the fire to blaze with a bright light for a short period.

My journal records: "I've enjoyed my time in the US but am looking forward to going home to see Simone. However I feel very sad that we're leaving tomorrow. I think that it's Del Valle, of all the places that we've stayed in the US, that it is my favourite site. It's so restful and peaceful, completely in tune with nature."

I rose early the next day and pottered around tidying and cleaning until Adam got up, no doubt disturbed by my activity. We left a few extra bits and pieces on the table next to the elderly couple's camper and headed for El Monte to return the RV, stopping at Emil Villa's for breakfast on the way. Adam's breakfast came on three large plates and consisted of two pancakes, two slices of French toast, three sausages, three rashers of bacon, two eggs and half a plate of hash browns. He ate it all!

At El Monte they gave me $145 (£85) back (three day's rental) and waived the cost of the propane that we'd used because of the trouble that we'd had. Like last year we had a bit of a wait for the shuttle bus to take us to the airport and spent the time looking around at the RVs for sale. We also had a four hour wait for our flight and spent the time sitting in an airport bar - drinking, eating and watching Portsmouth City Football Club play a match on the large screen TV!

The flight back was long, cramped and hot. Next time I'm going to insist on an aisle seat! Simone met us at the airport and then spent five minutes panicking because she'd lost the parking ticket that we needed to get out of the car park before we could set off!

The wanderers had returned home!

Chapter 21: Reminiscing
(With Apologies to Buddy Holly)

Adam and I had a fantastic time on both trips. We had some setbacks and some problems, but even more good times. We both gained a great deal from the trips in terms of cultural understanding, the experience of travelling through the extraordinary US countryside and the privilege of chatting and exchanging views with the local Americans that we met. Simone and my original intentions for the trip had been for Adam to have an educational, culturally enlightening and fun trip, and I believe that we achieved our aims. The problems we experienced, and the way that we overcame them, merely reinforced the educational and cultural aspects of the trips in my opinion.

When Adam was young he liked to ask us after a day out, "What was the best bit?" and "What was the worst bit?", "What would you change?"

So in answer to some of his now unspoken questions, the highlights of the trips (in order of preference) for me were:

- Yosemite
- Del Valle
- The helicopter flight over the Hoover Dam
- Being shown around San Francisco by Bob
- The scenery in general
- Visiting Alcatraz

Adam's top six (in his own words) were:

- The scenery
- The culture (or, more specifically the history of the amalgamation of many cultures and the result)
- Haight Ashbury
- The different geology and wildlife
- The obvious opportunities available to the population of America
- The weather

There are a few things that, with hindsight, I would change:
- I'd cover less miles so that we could spend more time 'looking and exploring' and less driving or preferably spend more time on the trip!
- I'd use a different RV rental company. They were fine about the refunds, but that doesn't replace the valuable time lost in getting the RV problems sorted out.
- I wouldn't rent a Sportster. I'd get something more comfortable - with a bit more power!

Adam would have liked to:
- Make the trip longer (a few months or even a year)
- Stay in each place longer

As I sit here writing, thinking back on our experiences, it occurs to me that in the whole of our travels we never met an American who had anything good to say about George W. Bush - so who voted for him? One man that I met at the hot springs in Tecopa, claimed that the previous election had been rigged; I don't know, but the people we met certainly were not happy with their president. The move away from US-produced goods to imported goods that I'd noted on the first trip, with regard to the cars on the road seemed to have continued and, on the second trip, I noticed that there were more imported drinks for sale in the shops and bars.

It seemed to me that America is divided into the 'haves' and the 'have nots'. Those in work seemed to have a good standard of living, with the latest gadgets and conveniences; however, there were a lot of beggars, especially in San Francisco, but they were also to be seen all over California. A big political issue whilst we were there during the second trip was that of granting citizenship to illegal immigrants, mostly Mexicans. Opinion seemed divided, but no one seemed in any doubt that the American economy would fail without this 'grey' market in labour. This seems a ridiculous state of affairs to me. The largest political and economic power on earth was (is?) dependent on illegal labour? In counterpoint to the internal problems of immigration, the economy and the external problems of American foreign policy, we found individual Americans to be engaging, friendly, interested in our opinions and helpful. We experienced a welcome, assistance where necessary and friendly interest from everyone that we met.

US bikers seem a little different from UK bikers. They are more into 'image' and 'lifestyle' than British riders, who are more interested in riding and the performance of their bikes. The emphasis on image and lifestyle borders on being a fashion statement. What it does mean is that not many US bikers wear serious safety and protective gear. Helmets are invariably of the 'skull cap' open face variety, not the full face helmets normally used in the UK, and leather trousers are almost unknown; thin leather chaps being the nearest some riders come to protecting their legs. As in the UK, the average age of riders is obviously increasing, with most riders being over fifty; however, there are more female riders in the US, often as part of a husband and wife pair. I'm not sure why this should be, but perhaps it is because the low centre of gravity and low seat height of a Harley makes it easier for people of a slight stature to ride. There are a few, younger sports bike riders on Japanese bikes, but they are in the minority.

When I first went to America 20 odd years ago, I was surprised at how law abiding the drivers were. Speed limits on Interstates were either 55 or 65 mph and everyone stuck to them. Now the speed limit is 70 in most places and most people seemed to be doing 80 plus; however, I think that the overall standard of driving is better, and more courteous than in the UK. This may be because I was in a large, and therefore intimidating RV though!

I don't know whether I'll ever go back to California, I'd like to very much, but there's a lot of world out there and I don't have the money or the time to visit it all. So next time I'll probably try another part of the world. Who knows, I might strike lucky and find somewhere I like as much as California!

Adam and I both enjoy travelling and exploring, but Simone doesn't like flying and exploring strange places, so any trip with her is likely to be more constrained. I, on the other hand, would like to go somewhere with an even greater cultural difference. Many people travel to 'see the sights' or to find 'guaranteed sun', but for me this is the minor part of the travel experience - it is the people and their food that I find most interesting. People across the world like travellers so it is not difficult to strike up a conversation with people you meet on your travels. I'd like to think that these meetings and exchange of ideas contribute in some small way to cultural understanding, and thus peace in our small world.

This book has been about the two trips we made to California. When we set out on the first trip, I had no intention of writing a book about it and only suggested to Adam that we should keep journals as I wanted him to have something to remember the trip by, and it fitted well with our educational objectives for the trip. I certainly had no idea that we would repeat the trip the following year. After reading my journal for the first trip when I got home, I started to formulate the idea of writing about our trip, but felt that it would have made for a relatively thin book and so shelved the idea. However, when we went on the second trip, the idea was still lurking in the back of my brain and so I recorded more detail in my journal.

During the Christmas festivities following our return, it occurred to me that I should write about both trips in one book. That way, if I could get it published, I could hopefully encourage other people to do more than simply book a foreign package holiday. If it's published, and you are still reading, I encourage you to go and look at the world without someone else telling you what you should see. The internet allows far greater opportunities than have been available in the past to research your destination and decide where you want to go and what you want to see. Make use of it!

Enjoy your travels! 'Go Your Own Way'![6]

---

6 With apologies to Fleetwood Mac!

Appendix I – Selected Recipes from the Trip

Buffalo Spaghetti Bolognese (four generous servings)
This is my take on an Italian classic. When finished the sauce should have a thick creamy texture to ensure that it coats all of the spaghetti strands.

Ingredients:
½ Kg/1 Lb minced buffalo (or best steak mince if you can't get buffalo)
4 rashers (approx 110 gms / 4 oz) diced smoked back bacon (or smoked lardons)
2 x tablespoons olive oil
1 x large or 2 x small onions roughly diced
2 x medium carrots
2 teaspoons dried basil
½ teaspoon dried oregano
½ teaspoon dried marjoram
garlic to taste (0 - 4 cloves)
3 x tins chopped tomatoes (choose the best as the juice is thicker and makes a better sauce!)
1 x large glass (300ml / 0.6 pint) red wine
2 x beef stock cubes
150 gms / 5½ oz tomato purée
dash of lemon juice
3 dashes dark soy sauce
1 x bunch (30 gms / 1 oz) fresh basil
300gms / 10 oz – 350 gms / 12 oz dried spaghetti
50 gm / 1¾ oz lump of fresh Parmesan cheese
salt and pepper

Method:
- If using bacon cut into small dice.
- Place mince on a chopping board and slice across the 'worms' at one centimetre / ½ inch intervals. Turn mince through 45 degrees and repeat.
- Roughly dice the onions and finely slice the carrots.

- Place a couple of tablespoons of olive oil in a metal casserole and heat until oil just starts to smoke.
- Add the mince and start to break up the lumps with a wooden spoon. Fry mince on high for two or three minutes before turning and adding the bacon. The mince and bacon will release water which must be evaporated off by continuing to break up the lumps and stirring until the mince is in separate 'grains'. When the water has evaporated the cooking sound will change to a 'sizzle' as the meat begins to fry. Continue frying and stirring for another five minutes then add the dried herbs and garlic (if used). Stir well and fry for another couple of minutes.
- Lower the heat to approximately one third and add the vegetables. Season with salt and pepper. Stir in with the meat and cover the pan. Stir every couple of minutes for ten minutes keeping the pan covered between stirrings.
- Add the chopped tomatoes, stir and raise the heat to full.
- Add a large glass of red wine.
- Add the beef stock cubes, tomato purée, a dash of lemon juice and three dashes dark soy sauce. Stir well and bring to the boil.
- Lower the heat to minimum, cover, and then gently simmer, stirring occasionally, for between 1 hour 15 min and 1 hour 30 min. If sauce starts to become too thick and dry add a little more red wine to loosen.
- About 15 min before the sauce is ready put a large pan of water on to boil for the spaghetti and finely grate the Parmesan into a serving bowl.
- Check the sauce's seasoning and adjust as necessary.
- Reserve four nice basil leaves for decoration and chop the remaining fresh basil (including the stalks). Add the chopped basil to the sauce and stir taking the sauce off the heat once stirred in.
- Add salt and a drop of olive oil to the boiling pasta water and then add the pasta. Cook until tender then drain well.
- Place a portion of spaghetti on each plate and spoon over a generous helping of sauce. Mix in with the spaghetti. Garnish with the reserved basil leaves and serve with the bowl of grated Parmesan on the side.

Chicken in a White Wine and Tarragon Sauce (two servings)

This essentially French dish is combined with spaghetti to make a satisfying and comforting meal.

Ingredients:
2 x chicken breasts
1 x tablespoon each of olive oil and butter for frying
1 x tablespoon of extra virgin olive oil for dressing the spaghetti
3 x sliced forestiere mushrooms (or the equivalent amount of portobello or button mushrooms)
1.5 x large glasses dry white wine
150 ml (3.5 fl oz) single cream
5 x sprigs fresh tarragon (or equivalent amount of dried tarragon)
1 x chicken stock cube
170 gms (6 oz) x dried spaghetti
135 gms (3 oz) x freshly grated parmesan cheese

Method:
- Melt the butter into the olive oil in an oven proof frying pan. When hot season both sides of the breasts with salt and pepper (if you use white pepper there won't be any black specks in the finished dish) and then fry the chicken breasts presentation side down.
- Once the breasts have taken on a nice colour, turn over and place the pan in a moderate oven (180C for fan oven 190C / Gas Mark 5).
- Cook for 20 – 30 mins until done. To test that the breasts are done place a metal skewer into the middle of the thickest part of the breast. Remove after 10 seconds and touch the tip to your top lip. If the skewer is hot the chicken is done.
- While the chicken is cooking bring a large pan of salted water to the boil.
- Once the chicken is cooked, cover with tin foil and put in a warm place to rest.
- Put the spaghetti in the boiling water to cook.
- Add the mushrooms to the chicken pan and cook until they start to soften.

- Add the white wine and stock cube to the pan and reduce by 50%.
- Add the cream to the pan and reduce by 50%.
- Add the tarragon and any juices from the resting chicken, take off the heat. Check and adjust seasoning if necessary.
- Check that the spaghetti is cooked; drain, toss in a little extra virgin olive oil and serve when it is. Slice each breast into three pieces and serve on top of the spaghetti.
- Spoon the sauce over the chicken and garnish with a tarragon leaf. Serve with the grated parmesan.

Pork Chops with Pasta and Cabbage (serves 2)
Pork, mustard, sage and cabbage, all made for each other!

Ingredients:
2 x Pork chops
4 x teaspoons English mustard
1 x bunch fresh sage (or 2 x teaspoons dried sage)
¼ x large savoy cabbage
100 gms (2.5 oz) x bacon lardons
75 ml (2.5 fl oz) x single cream
1 x glass dry white wine
1 x dash soy sauce
1 x 400gm (14 oz) pack of filled pasta (eg tortellini or ravioli)
2 x tablespoons fresh pork or chicken stock (or ½ x pork or chicken stock cube)
135 gms (3 oz) x freshly grated parmesan cheese

Method:
- Smear one teaspoon of mustard over each side of the chops, add salt and pepper and a generous pinch of sage. You can add a little crushed garlic as well if you like. You can also use other mustards (e.g. Wholegrain, Dijon etc.).
- Place the chops in a pre heated oven (190C fan oven / 200C / Gas Mark 6). Cook for around 25 mins or until done.
- Meanwhile shred the cabbage and fry the lardons in a wok or large frying pan. When they are two thirds done add the cabbage and fry. Do not stir too often as we want a little colour on the cabbage. Once the cabbage starts to wilt and has taken on some colour turn off the heat and add a dash of soy sauce and mix through.
- Bring a large pan of salted water to the boil and add the filled pasta. Bring back to the boil and cook for a further 3 mins (or according to the manufacturers instructions).
- Once the pork is cooked set aside to rest in a warm place. Deglaze the pan with the wine and reduce by 50%. Add the cream and a further generous pinch of sage along with a little pork stock (or half a pork stock cube). Reduce by 50%.
- Serve with the sauce over the pasta and a little grated parmesan.

Quesedillas

Quesedillas are the Mexican equivalent of cheese on toast and can be a simple snack or a meal in their own right depending of the fillings.

Ingredients:
140 gms (5 oz) x grated cheddar cheese (you can substitute your favourite melting cheese if you wish)
4 x 10-inch flour tortillas
225 gms (8 oz) x chopped cooked chicken
2 x green chillies
½ x chopped red pepper
2 tablespoons coarsely chopped fresh coriander

Method:
- Put a tortilla into a hot frying pan large enough to contain the tortilla. Sprinkle with half of the chicken, half of the coriander, and and half of the cheese.
- Top with a second tortilla and cook for about 3 minutes until the underside of the bottom tortilla is golden brown in several spots and half of the cheese is melted.
- Using a spatula, turn the quesadilla over and cook for a further 2 to 3 minutes until the underside of the second tortilla is crisp and golden brown in several spots and all of the cheese is melted. Remove from the pan and cut into wedges.
- Repeat to make a second quesadilla.

One Pot Chicken Casserole
Cooking the potatoes in with the casserole not only minimises washing up, but also allows them to take on the flavours of the casserole.

Ingredients:
2 x skinless chicken breasts cut into ¾ inch cubes
110 gms (4 oz) bacon lardons (or 3 rashers smoked back bacon cut into dice)
2 x dessert spoons flour + 1 dessert spoon mustard powder
1 x large onion (350 gms / 12 oz approx)
2 x medium carrots sliced
2 sticks celery, de-veined and finely sliced
1 x parsnip cut into even sized cubes
1 x teaspoon fresh chopped rosemary
1 x teaspoon fresh chopped sage
4 x cloves garlic, finely minced
4 x bay leaves
5 x medium potatoes (King Edwards or similar) peeled and quartered
750 ml (26 fl oz) chicken stock
Olive oil for frying

Method:
- Mix the four and mustard powder together with a little salt and pepper in a large polythene bag.
- Add the chicken pieces to the bag, close the top leaving plenty of free space in the bag and shake to evenly coat the chicken with the flour mixture.
- Heat the oil in a large thick bottomed saucepan or casserole dish and add the coated chicken, then the bacon lardons. Brown evenly on all sides over a high heat.
- Remove the meat from the pan with a slotted spoon and reserve.
- Add a little more oil if the pan is dry and turn the heat down. Add the prepared vegetables and garlic. Gently sweat until the onions are softened.

- Once the onions are soft add the rosemary and sage and cook for another two minutes.
- Add the stock and bring to the boil then add the bay leaves.
- Turn the heat down as low as it will go and cover the pan.
- Cook for about one hour, stirring gently occasionally.
- Add the potatoes to the pan and bring back to the boil. Cover and continue cooking over a low heat for a further 20 minutes. The casserole is ready when the potatoes are cooked.

Minted Lamb Chops with Crushed Garlic Potatoes and Peas

Crushing the potatoes with garlic and olive oil gives this dish a very Mediterranean feel.

Ingredients:
2 x Lamb chump chops
110gms (4 oz) finely chopped fresh mint
1 x dessert spoon white wine vinegar
3 x dessert spoons runny honey
450 gms (1lb) new potatoes
4 x tablespoons fresh or frozen peas
4 x minced garlic cloves
Extra virgin olive oil

Method:
- Combine the finely chopped mint, vinegar and honey.
- Place chops in a bowl and brush with the mint / vinegar and honey mixture.
- Cover and put in a fridge for at least two hours, preferably overnight, to marinade.
- Pre heat the oven to 190C fan oven / 200C / Gas Mark 6. Place chops on a baking tray and place in the oven.
- Cook for 30 mins, or until done (the actual time will depend on the size and thickness of the chops and how well you like your lamb cooked). Use any left over marinade to baste the chops during cooking.
- Meanwhile cook the potatoes in their skins until just done.
- Cook the peas, adding a teaspoon of salt and a teaspoon of sugar to the water. They only need a couple of minutes once the water is boiling.
- Crush the potatoes with a fork or potato masher. DON'T mash the potatoes! There should be some 'lumps' of un-mashed potato! Stir in the minced garlic and a good drizzle of olive oil.
- Serve with a sprig of mint as garnish.

Chilli Con Carne in Tortilla Wraps

Most people serve chilli with rice, but we like it in a tortilla wrap with a little sour cream and guacamole.

Ingredients:
1 x tbsp oil
1 x large onion
1 x red pepper
2 x garlic cloves
1 x level tsp hot chilli powder
1 x tsp paprika
1 x tsp ground cumin
500g (17 oz) lean minced beef
1 x beef stock cube
1 x 400g (14 oz) can chopped tomatoes
½ x tsp dried marjoram
1 tx sp sugar
2 x tbsp tomato purée
1 x 400g (14 oz) can red kidney beans
soured cream
guacamole
tortillas

Method:
- Prepare your vegetables. Chop your onion into small dice, about 5mm square.
- Cut your pepper in half lengthways, remove stalk and wash the seeds away, then chop.
- Heat the oil for 1-2 minutes until hot. Add the onions and cook, stirring fairly frequently, for about 5 minutes, or until the onions are soft and slightly translucent. Add the garlic, pepper, chilli, paprika and cumin. Stir, then leave it to cook for another 5 minutes, stirring occasionally.
- Turn the heat up and, when the pan is hot enough for the meat to sizzle add the meat to the pan breaking the lumps up with a wooden spoon. Cook for 5 minutes, until all the mince lumps have

broken down and it is uniformly brown. Keep the meat frying, not stewing!
- Dissolve the stock cube in 300ml/1/2 pint of hot water. Pour this into the pan with the mince mixture. Add the can of chopped tomatoes plus the marjoram and the sugar, if using (if using chocolate, put in when adding the beans), and add a good shake of salt and pepper. Squirt in about 2 tbsp of tomato purée and stir the sauce well.
- Bring to the boil, stir, cover and lower the heat until it is gently bubbling and leave for 20 minutes. Stir occasionally to make sure the sauce doesn't catch on the bottom of the pan or isn't drying out. If it is, add a couple of tablespoons of water and make sure that the heat really is low enough. After simmering gently, the saucy mince mixture should look thick, moist and juicy.
- Drain and rinse the beans and stir them into the chilli. Add chocolate. Bring to the boil again, and gently bubble without the lid for another 10 minutes, adding a little more water if it looks too dry. Taste a bit of the chilli and season. It will probably take a lot more seasoning than you think. Now replace the lid, turn off the heat and leave your chilli to stand for 10 minutes before serving.
- While the chilli is standing heat up your tortillas.
- Wrap two or three spoonfuls of chilli, a spoon of sour cream and a spoon of guacamole in each tortilla to serve.

Clam Chowder

At Fisherman's Wharf Adam and I had our chowder served in a hollowed out sourdough loaf. You can of course serve it in a traditional bowl if you wish!

Ingredients:
30 x clams
25g (1 oz) butter
50g (2 oz) x bacon lardons or sliced bacon, cut into small pieces
1 x small onion, diced finely
1 x carrot diced finely
225g (8 oz) x potatoes, diced but not washed
300ml (10 fl oz) x milk
120ml (4 fl oz) x cream
1 x bay leaf, crushed
cooking liquor from the clams
salt and pepper
1 x tbsp fresh parsley

Method:
- Wash and scrub the clams then place them in a large pan with a splash of water. Cover tightly and cook over a high heat. As soon as the clams are open, take the pan off the heat and drain them in a colander, saving the cooking liquor in a bowl. Remove the clams from their shells and cut the meat into small pieces.
- Fry the bacon in the butter until it starts to brown. Add the onions and fry until softened.
- Place the potatoes and carrots in a separate large pan with the milk, cream and bay leaf. Bring to the boil then reduce to a slow simmer until just cooked but still firm. Add the bacon, onions and clam cooking liquor and simmer for a further ten minutes then add the clams. Warm through then season with salt (if necessary) and freshly ground pepper.
- Serve and garnish with chopped fresh parsley.

Dijon Chicken

You can combine this dish with many things. Pasta, or potatoes cooked in your favourite way and veg. I had it with chips and peas in Yosemite but when I cook it for myself I like to have it with asparagus and boiled new potatoes, both tossed in a little butter.

Ingredients:
5 x tablespoons finely chopped fresh tarragon
4 x tablespoons Dijon mustard
4 x tablespoons dry white wine
1 x tablespoon olive oil
1 x tablespoon honey
2 x skinless chicken breasts

Method:
- Mix the mustard, wine, tarragon, oil and honey together to for a smooth marinade.
- Marinade chicken breasts in the mixture for at least two hours, preferably overnight.
- Place the marinaded chicken breasts on a baking tray and bake in a moderate oven (170C fan oven / 180C / Gas Mark 4) until the breasts are cooked through when the juices run clear and it is white all the way through with no pinkness. They should take around 30 mins to cook depending on size and thickness.
- When the breasts are nearly cooked heat up the remainder of the marinade and simmer gently for a two or three minutes to make a mustard sauce.
- To serve spoon the heated sauce over the chicken.

BBQ Chicken

The chicken is best cooked on a BBQ, but if this isn't available it can be cooked in the oven. As with the Dijon chicken above it was served with chips and peas, but this can be served with any of the accompaniments above, or just with a fresh salad.

Ingredients:
240g (8oz) x tomato tomato ketchup
120ml (4 fl oz) x water
120ml (4 fl oz) x apple cider vinegar
25g (1 oz) x light brown sugar
25g (1 oz) x caster sugar
1/4 x tbsp fresh ground black pepper
1/4 x tbsp onion powder
1/4 x tbsp ground mustard
1/2 x tbsp lemon juice
1/2 x tbsp Worcestershire sauce
2 x skinless chicken breasts

Method:
- Combine all ingredients except the chicken in a saucepan. Bring mixture to a boil, reduce heat to simmer. Cook uncovered, stirring frequently, for 1 hr.
- Make three slashes in each chicken breast and then cover with the BBQ sauce. Make sure the chicken breasts are fully coated. Marinade for at least two hours, or preferably overnight, reserving any leftover sauce.
- If using a BBQ cook the marinaded chicken over medium coals basting frequently with the reserved sauce.
- If cooking in the oven Place the marinaded chicken breasts on a baking tray and bake in a moderate oven (170C fan oven /180C/Gas Mark 4) until the breasts are cooked through. Baste frequently with the reserved sauce. They should take around 30 mins to cook depending on size and thickness.
- In either case the breasts are cooked through when the juices run clear and it is white all the way through with no pinkness.

Boef Borginonne

I like to use beef skirt for this instead of the more traditional shin as I believe it has more flavour.

Ingredients:
3 x tablespoons rapeseed oil
600 gms (21 oz) beef skirt
100 gms (3 oz) smoked bacon lardons
200 gms (6 oz) carrots cut into large chunks
200 gms (6 oz) shallots
200 gms (6 oz) chestnut or foristiere mushrooms
2 x cloves garlic
1 x bouquet garni
3 x bay leaves
1 x tablespoon tomato purée
1 x bottle good red wine

Method:
Heat the oil in a thick based casserole pan. Cut the skirt into large chunks and brown in the hot oil. Do this in batches so the pan doesn't cool too much when the meat is added. Remove the meat from the pan and reserve.

Brown the whole shallots, then remove and reserve.

Brown the lardons and carrots, adding the mushrooms and garlic a minute or two before adding the beef back to the pan.

Add the beef back to the pan including any juices that have come out of the meat. Then stir in the tomato purée.

Add the whole bottle of wine and around 100ml of water to the pan, season, and bring to the boil. Once boiling cover with aluminium foil cut to the size and shape of the pan. The foil should be resting directly on top of the bourginonne.

Place the pan in a cool oven (150C / 130C fan / gas mark 2). Cook for three to three and a half hours. Check and adjust seasoning if necessary.

Serve with mash and cabbage, not forgetting to remove the bay leaves first!.

Printed in Great Britain
by Amazon.co.uk, Ltd.,
Marston Gate.